The Last Apprentice

Life's journey of a baby boomer

by

Reg Stoddon

To Clementine
Best Wishes
Reg Stoddon

Typeset in Sabon LT Std

Design, typesetting and publishing by UK Book Publishing

www.ukbookpublishing.com

Cover design by Stephen Dixon

ISBN: 978-1-912183-19-7

Dedicated to my wife Jean for putting up with me, my business and all of the inconvenience that she has endured throughout our wonderful married life.

Foreword

During 1946 and 1947, most men who had served in the 1939 to 1945 war were demobilised and went home to their wives and families. With so many men being returned to their loved ones in a relatively short space of time and having been away for so long, the inevitable happened and for a period lasting two or three years after their return, the birth rate soared. The babies born during this period of time were and still are known as the 'Baby Boomers', of which I am one.

At that time rationing was still in force and some goods were harder to obtain than they had been during the war years. The children born a little earlier than ourselves, and of course their parents, had known better times and therefore knew that they were living a life of austerity, but to baby boomers like myself who had never known anything else, life in the beginning did not seem unusual. Shopping with ration books and searching for hard to find food and clothing was completely normal as was wearing hand me downs and second hand clothes.

The government of the day did its best by providing concentrated orange juice, dried milk and cod liver oil for all children to ensure that during these shortages, children got sufficient vitamins and nutrition to lead a reasonably healthy life. I liked all of them but the cod liver oil did not agree with me and used to make me vomit so I was no longer given it. My parents used to buy malt, which was administered to me on a teaspoon. I don't know whether or not it was on ration but somehow they got some and it was given to me for additional nutrition. After I started school I got one third of a pint of free milk every day and did so in fact for my entire time at school, which I am sure gave me an extra good start in life, so despite the shortages, in some respects we were better looked after than some poorer children are today.

Black marketing was rife, illegal and carried a severe punishment but my parents used to buy eggs from a farm a few miles away, when they received a letter in the post telling them that 'Auntie had finished knitting a jumper', signalling that there were some eggs going spare. They also got some black market milk by leaving the front door unlocked so the milkman could come inside and pour milk from his large jug into our smaller jug without been seen, therefore the neighbours could not monitor the quantity being delivered. That sadly stopped after the milkman was caught and heavily fined with the threat of a prison sentence for any future offence. It appears that he was helping a few of his customers, particularly those with young children, and one of our neighbours must have reported him to the police for black marketing. The saddest part of this sorry tale is that he was not profiteering but was selling any extra milk he had, at the ordinary price as he was genuinely trying to help the people whom he thought needed it most.

There were frequent power cuts which I remember well, until the infrastructure was restored and power stations destroyed by bombing were rebuilt. As there was also a severe shortage of coal at that time, it must have had an impact on how much electricity could be generated. Gas was an alternative but that too needed coal until natural gas came along several years later.

Here is the tale of one baby boomer and snippets from one life; it is not a complete autobiography or intended to be one. Much has been missed out but I hope that it gives a flavour of how baby boomers were born into times of great hardship, which eventually developed into the 'golden age' for most of us.

About Me

I am just an average person of my generation, so really my life is no more special than anyone else's. The inspiration for writing this has come from my late father-in-law, Tom Robinson, and at the request of various family members and friends.

Towards the end of Tom Robinson's life, he decided to write about his childhood in both England and New Zealand and subsequently about his adult life. Unfortunately during this process, his memory was not improving and many important features of his life were omitted whilst others were repeated. What he did write was fascinating though, and gave a good insight into what life was like from the beginning of the twentieth century up to the Second World War.

Whilst my writings will probably not interest many people at the present time, I do this in the hope that future generations might find my way of life as interesting as I have found reading about the lives of others who lived long before me and left records of the event. I am doing this now whilst my memory is reasonably fresh and hopefully am giving myself enough time to complete the process before I too expire or start to repeat myself!

Before I start, I feel it is important that the reader is aware of my background and where I come from. I have always been interested in family history and started studying it shortly after I was married in 1970. I do not intend to bore you with my complete family tree but it will be relevant to know about some of my ancestors. On my father's side they originated from near Belford in Northumberland through his mother, and Newport in Wales through his father. My mother was born Joy Mason and her maternal grandparents were from Bilsby in Lincolnshire and her paternal grandparents from Cork in Eire.

When I was born, my only grandparent still alive was my mother's mother. She was called Bertha Mason, born in 1884 and was the daughter of a clergymen and the granddaughter of a clergyman. She was educated at boarding school and became a governess when she started her working life. As a girl she had a privileged and well educated upbringing compared to most folks of that time, which in some ways impacted on my life as my granny worked tirelessly to have my mother privately educated. My mother was in fact illegitimate as my grandmother supposedly was the victim of a bigamous marriage to Edward O'Brien. My family history searches have failed to substantiate this, so it is possible that my grandmother was just another girl who became pregnant after a relationship, which in those days was socially unacceptable, especially with the consequences of an illegitimate baby. Getting caught out by a bigamous marriage carried a certain amount of sympathy and, whilst still carrying a stigma, was not as bad as being yet another unmarried mother.

My grandmother moved to London to distance herself from her siblings and other relatives, so as not to bring shame and embarrassment upon them. During her young childhood my mother was looked after by a succession of childminders until she started school, a private convent school paid for by my grandmother who by now had become a very successful door-to-door saleslady representing Goblin Vacuum Cleaners and later Kleez-eze products, supplemented by translating

French and German documents during the evenings. My grandmother had become fluent in both the French and German languages through her excellent boarding school education.

When my mother left school, she had a posh London accent and with her private education this stood her in good stead for the rest of her life. During 1941 she was evacuated to Lancaster with her work to escape the severe London bombing and then never lived anywhere else for the rest of her life.

My father Walter Lyndon Stoddon (Lyn) was born in Whitley Bay, Tyne and Wear (Northumberland until 1974). His father, my grandfather, had moved from his birthplace in Newport, Wales, married my grandmother and his occupation was teaching, playing and composing music in his new location. My father seemingly also had an unconventional upbringing from an eccentric father, and loving mother who died when he was just 20 years old. During the 1920s my father had learned to fly aircraft, which enabled him to become a test pilot during the 1930s, ultimately leading to him joining the Royal Air Force in 1939 at the start of the Second World War. He ended up being stationed at Morecambe during 1945 where he met my mother at a dance, and the rest, including me, is history.

I have never kept a diary so the dates of many of my early memories are approximations, becoming more accurate as time goes by. My memories start from the late 1940s, increasing during the 1950s through to the 1960s when I started work and then on to 1980.

The 1960s are famously called The Swinging Sixties when youngsters were liberated and there was supposedly free sex and the beginning of mass drug taking. Not for me! I didn't get offered many drugs and even less sex; there was the odd teenage grope here and there but that was about it. I mention it here rather than later as I do not intend to go into any sordid details about who did what and where and with whom. There is only the odd exception, as many people that

I mention are still alive and plenty of them are now pillars of society, respectable and married. I do not want to be the cause of any marital discord through their foolishness of youth or my careless words. I am not ashamed to admit that until my wife came along I did not have a full sexual relationship with any girl, so hopefully will not be blamed for any break ups through my writings. I did have and still do have a strong religious conviction in that department, particularly for the young starting out in life. I do not judge others or lecture on the rights and wrongs of that issue but can only say what is comfortable for me. I saved myself for my wife because of my religious beliefs and have absolutely no regrets in doing so. I am a Christian but now no longer a regular churchgoer as I have seen so much corruption within most organised religion that I cannot bring myself to endorse it by regular church attendance. This saddens me as I found friendship and fellowship amongst my fellow Christians and also many of the clergy, but cannot condone some modern changes that have slowly crept in to most branches of organised religion during the last forty years. I might be completely wrong and it might be me that is the sinner for not joining in with fellow believers, but my conscience will not allow me to do so.

As previously stated, these writings will cover my life until 1980 and describe the many people who affected my life and how things gradually changed for all of us, taking us from severe austerity to relative prosperity. I may write another book in the future to continue my journey but on the advice of my family am stopping here for the time being, owing to the size of this one!

1946 to 1951

I was born in the Royal Lancaster Infirmary on 4th October 1946. I understand that the country was enjoying an Indian summer and that it was unusually hot for that time of year. My parents were living in rented accommodation at 45 Portland Street, Lancaster, which they subsequently started buying for the princely sum of £650. My father's brother, my Uncle Archie, was staying that night as he was passing through Lancaster on his way home to Northumberland from a visit somewhere further south, and shortly after tea my mother's waters broke so she quickly ended up giving birth to me at approximately 7.15pm. In those days childbirth was a two week affair, with the actual birth being in hospital for those who could afford it and the remainder of time convalescing and getting used to looking after the baby. Until then my mother had savings but completely used them up having me, as the National Health Service didn't come along until shortly after I was born. By the time that she came home winter had set in and the weather had become very cold.

My very earliest memories were lying still, not being able to move and looking at the sun shining on plain light green wallpaper. When it went dull I was sad and when it went bright I was happy. I can only have been a few months old as I could not stand up or move very far but later I verified that my cot was in a position where that wall that I observed caught the sun by mid to late morning. I remember nothing else clearly until I was about two or maybe three years old. Whilst I was still sleeping in a cot, I am told that I used to stand up and rattle it so vigorously that I could make it travel around the room. My father found a way of fastening it to the wooden skirting board to prevent this but because I kept trying to move it, I had shaken the joints loose. One night my parents heard an almighty crash, rushed upstairs and found me fast asleep with my cot in pieces lying on top of me. They were amazed that I could have slept through that, and to this day I am a very heavy sleeper. I can remember being pushed around in a sort of pram-cum-pushchair contraption in the rain and getting wet, as in those days there were no plastic see through covers to keep kids dry. My mother had been trying to get coal but as it was on ration she had great difficulty, despite trailing round several coal merchants.

My granny, Bertha Mason, my mother's mother, always came for a few days each year to spend Christmas with us. In 1948, I had a very nasty chill which was threatening to turn to pneumonia whilst my granny was staying with us. My mother did not know what to do but my granny suggested that a teaspoon of brandy every few hours might be beneficial. This was an expense that my mother could have done without but nevertheless she bought a small bottle of brandy, probably the equivalent of about 175cl today. Over the next day or two I was responding favourably and was sleeping in my parents' double bed with the brandy on the bedroom mantelpiece. My mother had left me asleep for a while and on one of her frequent checks was horrified to find me still fast asleep with the empty brandy bottle on the bed beside me. She did not know what to do but my granny advised her to leave me to sleep it off and predicted that when I woke up there would probably be a significant improvement. I slept for a long time and when I awoke, the worst was indeed over and I recovered quickly.

I also remember our dear old next door neighbour Mrs Crombleholme from number 47 who doted on me as a child. She had no children of her own and used to invite me into her house to bang on her lovely piano and to spoil me. She occasionally gave me oranges which were almost impossible to get for several years after the Second World War and my mother dared not tell her that I hated fruit and refused everything except bananas which were even more difficult to obtain. I remember going in a car with her and Mr Crombleholme to Liverpool to see their married nephew. I don't remember the whole day but I do remember parts, as it was probably the first time that I had been away from my parents for a whole day. It would have been the longest car ride that I had ever had, about sixty miles each way, but with no motorways and having to drive through every town centre to get there and back, it would have been an epic journey.

A very clear memory that I have was getting ready for a treat to be taken to Morecambe for an afternoon at the seaside. This I loved but just before setting off, I fell down the full flight of our cellar steps and ended up with a nasty gash over my left eyebrow. I was rushed to the doctor who managed to stop the bleeding but all that I was interested in was getting to Morecambe. I think that my mother felt so sorry for me that she still took me, as I was so upset at the prospect of missing the trip. I still have a slight scar from that episode which is visible to those who look for it.

About this time I had a bad tooth. I cannot imagine why as there was a sugar ration in place and I did not get the opportunity to consume many sweets. I had my first visit to the dentist, Mr Cardwell in Marketgate, Lancaster and my mother was told that the tooth would have to be removed. She was also asked to leave the surgery whilst the procedure took place. She returned to the waiting room and only moments later heard an almighty yell, which was from me. It appears that as it was only a milk tooth, the dentist had decided to whip it out quickly without any form of anaesthetic or pain relief. My mother was furious with the dentist and told him so but as a result I was so afraid of dentists that I never went back to one until about eight years later. It was about this time that I had a bout of wanting to see more of the outside world and had many attempts at escaping from home to go out and see the world. My first attempt was highly successful and I remember making it to Lancaster Castle Railway Station, which even for an adult is a good ten minute walk from Portland Street. I had been there several times before with my dad who used to get a platform ticket so that I could watch the trains, all steam in those days. I remember evading the ticket collector and waiting for him to be distracted before walking past the barrier and onto the platform. I got into a railway carriage waiting at the platform from where the Morecambe train usually left and hid under a seat. Shortly afterwards a man got into the carriage, spotted me, called the guard and I was apprehended till my dad picked me up to take me home. It turned out that the train was the Glasgow Express and five minutes later, I would have been on my way to Scotland. My mother had been frantic with worry, the neighbours had all been looking for me and the police had been informed. After I arrived home I received what I remember as the first of many physical punishments that I would receive over the next few years, or as my mother put it, 'A damn good thrashing'!

I had now been branded as an escapologist so an alarm system was fitted. At the top of the rear of our front door on the hinge side, a metal plate was screwed on and on the door frame a spring clip was fastened. When the door was opened even slightly, the clip touched the metal plate and when connected to the doorbell circuit, an electrical connection was made, ringing the doorbell. Under the spring clip a small on/off switch was situated so that my parents could reach up to switch off the alarm if they wanted to come and go but the switch was placed high enough, so that I could not reach it. It was all in vain as shortly afterwards, when my mum was hanging out washing in the back yard, I pulled a dining chair down our hallway to the back of the front door, climbed up on it, switched off the alarm and I was away. This time I was found by the police in the Stonewell area of Lancaster, about a 15 minute walk away and at the opposite end of town from where I lived. I must have crossed several main roads to get there but don't remember much about it. My mum was not amused when she found that the police, instead of intimidating me, had fed me with biscuits at the police station pending her arrival, but when I got home there was a lot of shouting and another good thrashing. On the third occasion, I climbed over the back yard wall but only got as far as Queen Street, two streets away. My mum had missed me quite quickly so had gone tearing off and found me herself, which resulted in more shouting and another good thrashing. I remember quite clearly my last escape attempt but not how I got away. I ended up at Dallas Road School to be with all of the other kids, which was only a couple of streets away. I don't remember the consequences of that but it would almost certainly be the customary good thrashing.

Clocks and watches always fascinated me and I constantly kept asking my parents the time, often several times every hour. They patiently kept telling me and even encouraged me by letting me dismantle old alarm clocks. At the age of three years old I learnt to tell the time perfectly to the great disbelief of a near neighbour called George West who was in fact a clockmaker. One day he asked my parents if he could ask me into his house, which he did. He stood me in front of the clock on his mantelpiece, kept altering the hands and asking me what time they showed. To his astonishment I was one hundred per cent perfect but he was dismayed that his eldest daughter Anita, who was twice my age, still could not tell the time.

I think that my mother realised that I needed the company of other children, so I was encouraged to have little friends – one was David Rack, the other Judith Hodgson. Both were neighbours' children whom I am still very friendly with to this day. This did the trick and my mother realised that I was a social animal suffering from boredom. Once I had friends, my escaping ambitions evaporated and eventually I was allowed to play outside with them and became a reformed character. Other children from slightly further up the street eventually joined us so we became quite a little gang.

At the age of four, I had my first holiday. My parents took me to Whitley Bay and we stayed with my dad's brother, Uncle Archie, and his wife Auntie Dora at my dad's old family home at 4 Edwards Road. It was a big house compared to ours and there seemed to be a lot of family there at the time. I met my cousins Reg (then known as Rex) and George who must both still have been living at home and would have been in their late teens or early twenties. The first morning after our arrival there, I had got up and gone down to the kitchen on my own. I was found by these cousins, munching my way through a packet of dog biscuits much to their amusement. Peter the dog must have gone short that week! My cousins then somehow acquired my clothes, dressed me and I remember clearly feeling uncomfortable after I was dressed. When my mother appeared she took off my trousers and re-dressed me, as my cousins, now creased up with laughter, had put my trousers on me the wrong way round. I never found out whether or not this was done on purpose but it could have easily been so, as they were both full of fun and were big practical jokers. I enjoyed the laughter and the banter as it was the very first time that I had experienced the company of my larger family. I was also taken to a newsagent's shop on Whitley Road owned and run by my Auntie Doris, my dad's sister. Her husband, my Uncle Jimmy Pollard Smith, worked as a signalman, just outside Monkseaton Station in the signal box (now part of the Newcastle Metro with the signal box long gone) and they had one son, my cousin Ian, an apprentice locomotive engineer at the Robert Stephenson Works in Newcastle upon Tyne, put on hold whilst he was doing his national service in the Royal Air Force.

From when I was a baby, my cousin Kath, the sister of George and Reg, had been a frequent visitor at our house. Her husband Oswald Slater of only a few months had died of tuberculosis and I, her new baby cousin was a beneficial distraction to her. As time went by during the later 1940s she continued to visit with her now new partner Eric Race who my parents did not like but I adored. He was a big man who had to duck under the house doorways and to me was a gentle giant. He taught me how to say my prayers at night and used to read me stories. He is the father of my second cousin Susan but more of that later as he and my cousin Kath never married; even in the 1940s and 50s there was a strong social stigma of unmarried couples living together.

During the late 1940s my dad was working as a cellulose sprayer for a local garage and my mum a part time cinema usherette, but there was still not enough money coming in to raise a family, pay the bills and keep up with the mortgage. My parents decided to take in lodgers who occupied our front room, which had now been kitted out with a bed settee. The first ones were a couple called Jock and Rene Skene who had a daughter twelve days younger than me called Marise. Marise, however, lived with her grandparents during the week whilst her parents worked but sometimes came for the weekend to be with her parents. My mum always seemed to get along well with the lodgers but not so my dad. He seemed to resent them, which resulted in rows between my parents.

It was about that time that I first became aware of what a camera was. My dad had purchased a Zeiss Super Ikonta camera on a trip to Germany shortly before the outbreak of the Second World War and the first time that I noticed it was when I was about the age of three. He and I walked to a local beauty spot called Ripley Heights and he took my picture. From that moment I wanted a camera and was hooked from that day to this on photography. I could not at that time, however, understand why the picture was not immediate and the concept of having to process the film.

When I was about four years old, Mary Hodgson, my friend Judith's mum, took Judith and me to King Street to watch His Majesty George VI drive through Lancaster. Everyone was cheering and waving union flags but the whole affair was over in seconds and I don't remember seeing the King although I did see his car.

My sister Marilyn was born on the 17th July 1951 and my dad and I went in a taxi to pick her and my mum up from the convalescent home to bring them back home about two weeks later. I was very pleased to have a baby sister and tried to help my mum as best as possible, although, looking back, I was probably more of a hindrance than a help.

Shortly after that I started at Dallas Road County Primary School early in September 1951. I had been taken to school the day before I started to show me which entrance to use and where to hang my coat, which was on a hook identified with the coloured sticker of a jack-in-a-box above it. The day on which I started school was chaotic. There were about forty pupils starting, with an almost equal mix of girls and boys. After our parents had left, some of the children started crying until eventually nearly every child was crying except me. This was a moment that I had waited for and I did not know what the fuss was all about, but did feel slightly intimidated surrounded by all of the wailing. After a few days everything settled down and formal lessons started. Our teacher was an elderly lady called Miss Dobson who was near retirement and was totally unsuited to teach a reception class. She was impatient, quick to anger and inflicted punishment at the drop of a hat. If a pupil asked to go to the toilet during lessons, the request was always refused, which resulted in many toilet accidents by most pupils at some stage or other. After the accident had occurred you would be dragged off to the toilet as a damage limitation exercise but by then of course it was far too late. If a pupil fell ill in class, they were not taken seriously and I remember one boy called David Cragg violently vomiting and making one hell of a mess. When being taught how to write, one had to do it right handed which was a problem for me, being at that time a natural left hander. We had to write with a piece of chalk on a miniature blackboard but whenever I had the chalk in my left hand, my hand was slapped, the chalk pulled out and placed into my right hand until I eventually conformed. I also remember a roaring coal fire in the classroom fireplace as the weather became colder.

Around that time I succumbed to a long succession of childhood illnesses such as measles, chicken pox, scarlet fever, mumps and whooping cough. The only thing that I never caught was German measles. This resulted in me missing a lot of my first year at school through illness but at least got me out of the clutches of Miss Dobson, of whom the whole class were afraid.

The Christmas of 1951 I remember very well. My granny was expected to arrive and she always came by taxi from the railway station and I was looking forward to seeing her. For some reason she was very late and my mother was beside herself with worry. My baby sister was asleep in her pram in the living room and eventually my mother could wait no longer. She gave me a pep talk and impressed upon me the very responsible task I had to perform. That was not to take my eyes off my baby sister whilst she went to the railway station and if anything seemed to be wrong, to immediately find a neighbour to help me. She said that she would only be a few minutes and would get back as soon as possible, then she went. I took my task most seriously and stood guard over Marilyn. Probably only about five minutes later, there was a knock at the front door which was a taxi driver with my granny emerging from the taxi. I explained that my mum had gone looking for her and shortly afterwards my red-faced, breathless mother re-appeared and all was well. During that Christmas time, my granny amused me by teaching me to play the snakes and ladders board game and tiddlywinks amongst other amusements. My granny only ever came for a few days over Christmas, so soon it was time for her to go and I remember feeling sad as I had reached an age when I was beginning to have a rapport with her and, I think, she with me.

1952 to 1953

When I left the reception class at school, I moved to the second class, taught by another elderly lady called Miss Wadeson. She was like a breath of fresh air though, and was everything that Miss Dobson was not, being kind, patient and understanding, making going to school a pleasure. There was a problem with me, however, as my reading was not coming on and I was behind most of the class in that department. My parents knew that I was not backward in that I had taught myself to tell the time fluently at the age of three and was not struggling with numbers but words were a problem. It was probably down to all the schooling that I had missed earlier because of the succession of illnesses and being turned into a right hander, but even when I had moved up to the next class taught by Miss Fort, I still was not reading. Enough was enough for my mother who decided that this had to be dealt with in her way. One weekend a blackboard was set up at home and an old book from my mother's schooldays was produced called 'Reading without tears'. Nothing could have been further from the truth as with a stick in one hand and the chalk in the other, I was made to start the book and was hit every time I could not read a word. There were indeed lots of tears as my mother kept chalking the words on the blackboard and hitting me with the stick until I got them right.

Once I got the hang of what reading was all about, I came along quite quickly as I enjoyed the new world that books were opening up to me. Television in Lancaster was just starting up but it would be years before we got one, so reading and the radio were my main sources of entertainment.

On Wednesday 6th February 1952 I must have been at home and off school as I remember that my mother was unable to access any radio programmes. Eventually she went to the front door, probably to see if the milk had arrived, to find that several neighbours were chatting to each other from their doorways. It turned out that our King, His Majesty George the Sixth, had died during the night and that Elizabeth his daughter was now our Queen. There was solemn music all day on the radio interspersed with occasional news broadcasts about the king's death and royal events as they were unfolding.

For my birthday my parents gave me a two wheeler bicycle and, although it was second hand, I was delighted. I couldn't ride it but my dad said that he would teach me and I was impatient to get started. My friend David Rack had never learnt to ride one either, so for three nights running we all went down to Dallas Road where my dad got us quickly up to speed. We had to use Dallas Road, as at that time it was the only quiet road in the area that was smooth with a good surface. Most other streets were still cobbled and trying to learn to ride on a very bumpy surface would have been more difficult.

The rest of 1952 must have been uneventful for me as except for school I don't have many memories, but I do remember Christmas particularly well as it was the last one that I enjoyed with my granny. She arrived as usual just before Christmas and played with me pretty well the whole of the time that she stayed. She taught me about money (pounds, shillings and pence in those days) and about the different value of coins. She had brought me a railway game for Christmas, which I loved to play with her. It listed every station between London to Glasgow and had small metal railway engines to move along the board. You threw a dice to progress the journey and in certain places had to wait for so many throws or go back to simulate all of the travelling problems that one might encounter. All too soon my granny had to go home and for the first and last time as it turned out, I went with my parents to see her off at Lancaster Castle Station. I remember that morning so distinctly, it was a gloomy winter morning, probably cold although I did not notice, and eventually the train left with my granny waving to us through the window at which she was seated. We walked as far as we could to the end of the platform still waving, until my granny and the train were going out of sight, passing the gantry of semaphore signals at the point where the platform ended. That is the very last memory that I had of my beloved granny as she died the following September.

1953 was a pretty exciting year as we were progressively being exposed to Coronation fever. It was slightly marred in March by the death of Queen Mary, the Queen's grandmother, but after that everything was about the forthcoming Coronation. One day when I was playing in the front garden of my friend Judith Hodgson, a van turned up, a large contraption was laid out on their front lawn and ladders were put against the wall of the house. I enquired as to what was going on and was told that a television aerial was being fitted to the chimney stack. I asked what television was and shortly afterwards was shown the set, still not switched on. I was told that one could see pictures on the set when it was working so waited for the switch on. Eventually it was working and my eyes almost popped out when I realised that these were moving pictures, albeit black and white and only on a twelve inch screen. I thought that this was fantastic despite the snowstorm that interrupted the picture whenever a vehicle drove past the house or if a neighbour happened to be using an electrical appliance. Little did I know on that fateful day how much this newly discovered invention (to me) would change and influence all of our lives forever. Coronation fever was now gripping the country and most houses had a model coach and horses or a portrait of the Queen in their front windows. All of the newspapers, magazines and periodicals seemed to have special editions or pull-out supplements and soon Coronation Day, June 2nd 1953, was upon us. In Lancaster this was a gloomy but dry day; it had rained heavily the day before but for us Coronation Day was dry. I was fortunate to watch most of the Coronation on television as Judith's mum and dad had said that I, along with several other neighbours, could go to their house to share the Coronation experience. Although only six years old, I understood most of what was going on and remember much of that day as if it were yesterday.

It was around that time that I first came across my Auntie Dolly; in reality she was the cousin of my dad and was a trained actress. I can remember sitting on the front step outside our house and a strange lady complete with her dog in tow ringing our doorbell, which my mum answered. After she and my mum had chatted, she was introduced to me as my Aunty Dolly; her dog, an ex- circus dog, was called Judy. She had come with a shopping bag from which she removed a couple of catering size jars of Bovril and a large quantity of Melba Toast. I liked Bovril but we did not usually see much, so found it amazing to have about a year's supply in the house all at once. It turned out that Aunty Dolly was working for Bovril as a demonstrator and these were samples, which she had almost certainly misappropriated from her employers. Before she left she gave me sixpence, which doubled my pocket money for that week. I had to earn my pocket money by going to the shop every day to pick up groceries. My mother had an account with the shop and used to send me with a list written in a red order book, which the shop used to price and return to me to give back to my mother. At the end of each week, my mother used to go to the shop to settle the account and hand over the relevant quota of ration coupons. My mother would shop in town for fresh food such as meat and fish, as and when we needed it, because few people in those days had refrigerators. That was the only way of ensuring that food did not have time to go off. Many groceries such as sugar and raisins were not pre-packed but the grocer would open one of many drawers on the wall behind the counter and with a metal scoop fill and weigh a thick blue paper bag and neatly fold it, tucking in the top flap in such a way that it would not accidentally open.

Around that time we had a change of lodgers, the Skenes went and the Partridges arrived: Jack and Sylvia and their three year old son, Michael. My mum instantly took to this family as they were dependable, reliable and hard-working people; Sylvia in fact remained a lifelong friend of my mum. In September disaster struck, my granny had become very ill and was in hospital. My mum had to go to London but when she got there my granny was so ill that she hardly recognised my mum and died of bowel cancer on September 10th. My dad went off to join my mum so Marilyn and I were looked after by Jack and Sylvia Partridge whilst my parents were away, arranging and attending the funeral. Before they returned my sister Marilyn broke out in a mysterious rash, the doctor was called and she was taken by ambulance to the isolation unit in Lancaster Beaumont Hospital with suspected smallpox. When my parents eventually arrived back they rushed off to the hospital but could only observe Marilyn through a small window. After a few days all was well as the doctors realised that she had been subject to insect bites and had reacted badly giving smallpox-like symptoms. My mum never really came to terms with the death of her mother and broke the news to me in a very cold and matter of fact way whilst cooking the dinner. She looked down at me and said, 'We had to go to London because your Granny has just died', then carried on making the dinner. I know now that this was her way of trying to deal with the situation as she must have been very upset and could not bear to talk at length about it, but even at six years old I had some concept of death and knew that I would not be seeing my granny again. Later in the afternoon I went to my parents' bedroom, lay on their bed and cried myself to sleep.

The following month was my seventh birthday although I don't remember much about it or about the Christmas that followed as this was no longer the momentous occasion that it had been in the past, now that my granny was no longer around.

The one thing that I do remember, however, was November 5th and the preparations for bonfire night. During the October break from school, various friends and I were collecting bonfire wood and taking it down to Dallas Road to the old drill hall site (now Ushers Meadow) to make a bonfire. On the way down to the site my friends taught me my very first rude song sung to the hymn tune 'There is a happy land' and it went as follows: '*There is a happy land far, far away, Where little piggies run three times a day, Wait until the butcher comes then you'll see those piggies run, Three slices off their bums, Three times a day*'. I did not dare sing it back at home though, as I knew that my parents would not approve and it would probably have resulted in the customary good thrashing if I had decided to try it out there. This was probably the beginning of my appreciation of mild vulgarity and innuendo, another turning point of my life.

1954

I remember little about this time, probably as nothing momentous was happening for me. Wartime rationing had, however, come to an end and I remember my parents being very excited about being able to buy goods freely and without coupons, with products which I had never seen before arriving in the shops. Our local grocery shop, 'Seeds' at the end of Queen Street, had received a small consignment of tinned salmon in small, medium and large sizes. To be fair to all of their customers, they had a lottery to decide the size of tin that you could purchase and I represented our family in picking out the ticket which was for a medium size tin. My parents were delighted that it was not a small tin, so for tea the following day we had a salmon salad. I had never had any sort of salmon before so really enjoyed the tinned salmon and have never forgotten how good it tasted. Although still on ration, coal was now also more available so my mum was no longer trailing round coal merchants trying to find enough coal to keep warm. There was a feeling that everything was getting better although I had never realised that anything was abnormal before, having lived my whole life with rationing and never knowing any different.

Kath and Eric were still together and made periodic visits to stay with us and I was always very excited when they arrived. My mum and dad did not share my enthusiasm, however, as they were still not married and my parents disapproved of the situation.

At school by now I was making better progress and was in Miss Robinson's class, a young, good looking teacher who made learning interesting. This class was called the transition class where one's future would be decided for streaming until the age of eleven and shortly afterwards I ended up in Class 1A of the Junior School with Miss Towler.

Miss Towler must have been pretty young although to me at the time that did not seem the case. She was very methodical, strict, demanded a high standard and made you work. She was, however, very fair and was well liked by most of her pupils. I was doing fine at school now and reading a lot in my spare time but my mother, concerned for my educational progress, made an impromptu visit one day to see my teacher, telling her to give me a damn good thrashing if I did not work. Miss Towler was impressed, as she had recently had two complaints from parents whose daughters could not cope with the strict regime and told my mother that I would get her favourable attention. Now I was in the Juniors, I felt that I was growing up and was being given a certain amount of freedom both at school and at home.

I spent a lot of my spare time playing with my friend David Rack who was still living with his parents and granny at 44 Portland Street, or with Judith Hodgson just round the corner at 3 Portland Place. David's dad had a car and if they had a weekend outing they often took me with them to give David some company. I liked going to Judith's house, however, as they had the television set which I enjoyed watching.

I don't remember specifically my eighth birthday or Christmas but I think at this time I was allowed to stay up until midnight on New Year's Eve to let in the New Year. This became a very important family tradition, as my dad, being a Geordie, held in very high esteem the rituals of bringing coal into the house through the front door at midnight and after putting it on the fire, opening the back door to let out the old year.

1955

Being now an eight year old, I was beginning to participate in more social activities. I can remember round about February, the school distributing small booklets from 'Doctor Barnardo's Homes', a charity caring for orphan children. Each tear out page in the booklet titled 'Sunny Smiles' had the picture of an orphan child which you sold, put the purchaser's name and what they had paid on a stub, and carried on until all of the pictures had been sold. The stubs and cash were returned to the school, who presented the proceeds along with other schools to a well-known celebrity at a gala night held at The Ashton Hall, Lancaster. Judith's mum took Judith and me to this gala night where Harry Corbett and Sooty his bear puppet were appearing. They were well known TV personalities but I could not see much, owing to so many taller people sitting in front of me, so it was a disappointing night.

I cannot think of many other things that happened until the beginning of my school holidays in July. This coincided with Kath and Eric descending on us and staying for a few days and shortly before they left, I was invited to return to Northumberland with them to stay for a month. I jumped at this offer and begged my parents to let me go, which, after some deliberation, they did. What an adventure this was for me as they were living in an old rambling house just south of Belford in Northumberland called 'High Mousen'.

We eventually arrived at Mousen at dusk. We had stopped at a farm just before we arrived to pick up some milk, which was still warm from the cow and for the first time in my life I had milk so fresh that it hadn't had time to cool down. Mousen had no mains electricity so oil lamps were lit and I was shown to my bedroom by a nightlight, which was blown out after I was safely tucked up in bed to prevent accidents. When I awoke the following morning, it was a lovely sunny day with daylight streaming in through my bedroom window. I got dressed and went downstairs and was given a conducted tour around the house. The large back downstairs room is where we lived and the front room was where their dogs lived. There were four: Ricky, a happy go lucky golden retriever; Lassie, a middle aged, good tempered German Shepherd (called an Alsatian in those days); her son Panther, a bad tempered, young, completely black dog; and Flash, an evil and dangerous German Shepherd to anyone who was not used to him. I was warned never to enter the front room on my own and after seeing Flash and Panther there was no chance that I was going to disobey that warning. Not only did the house not have electricity but it was not connected to the mains water supply. The house was, however, fully plumbed with toilets, sinks and a bath, there was also a coal boiler in the kitchen if hot water was required. Water was gravity fed into the plumbing from a large tank situated in the attic of the house, which was filled from a natural spring. A petrol driven pump in an outside building pumped the water from the spring to the top of the house and a crude wooden bar moved down the outside wall as the tank was filling. When the bar reached a certain point on the wall, the tank was full and the pump had to be stopped to prevent the tank from overflowing. Water was therefore precious and had to be used very sparingly, so much so that I only had a bath once whilst I was there and even then, the water level was very shallow. Toilet flushing had also to be economical with multiple sessions per flush except when one had been for a longer stay, then one flush per session was permitted. I soon got into the routine of this Spartan existence and amused myself playing in the garden by the side of the house and behind the trees on the driveway. Lassie and Ricky were good company and only being small for my age, I used to ride on Ricky until Kath spotted me, then that was stopped. Ricky being a big dog didn't seem to mind but I was forbidden to do it again. The one thing I really missed was the radio as there were no transistor radios then but just one large portable one that ran off wet accumulators. Eric got these charged up but warned me to only use them sparingly as they didn't last long. They didn't as I could not bear to switch the radio off and after only a few hours everything stopped working. Eric decided not to bother again as I had not been careful, so that was my listening curtailed for the duration.

We had a couple of shopping trips to Alnwick. On the first occasion they left me in the car for a few minutes whilst they shopped but on the second occasion, I was allowed out and into what I think was Woolworths. They bought me a plastic battleship that fired torpedoes, which kept me amused back at Mousen. They filled a large sink with their precious water, albeit cold, but it kept me busy for hours whilst I happily played at sea battles and fired my torpedoes.

One evening Eric had to go and see a customer and Kath and I went with him. He was an Agricultural Representative for Massey Ferguson and sold tractors. I remember him driving us along country lanes and then through tracks in fields. There were a couple of farm gates that we had to open and close, so I had to get out of the car to do this job. Eventually we arrived at a farmhouse, which obviously had no mains electricity as the farmer's wife was ironing clothes with two flat irons. There was a large metal range type fire surround with a roaring fire in the grate, with one iron perched alongside it heating up, whilst the lady was ironing with the second iron. When that cooled down, the irons were switched so that she always had a hot iron in use. Eventually it was getting dark and oil lamps were lit so by the time that we left it was completely dark. I did not fancy getting in and out of the car twice on a dark night to open and shut the gates, so I pretended to fall asleep almost immediately after setting off on the return journey, which meant that Kath had to do it instead.

On another evening we went on a trip to Morpeth to see relatives whom I had never met, Frank and Doris Lyndon and their grown up children Robbie and his sister Dorothy. We had tea there and Robbie showed me a working model submarine made in wood that he had built. Before we left he gave it to me and showed me in his kitchen sink how it worked. I was very excited when we left as I now had something to torpedo with my battleship. A few days later Doris Lyndon and Dorothy came to tea at Mousen. It was a lovely summer afternoon and as there was no car involved, they must have come on the bus and walked the half mile or so from the main road up to the house. We had lovely white serviettes, which had been brought out especially for the occasion and reminded me of a little trick that had been shown to me by my schoolmates with a story that accompanied it. I cannot remember the exact dialogue but it involved folding the serviette in lots of different ways, each way to resemble a different item. The final punchline was to fold the serviette and pull the four corners so that two areas popped out to resemble a brassiere. This I did and proudly held it up to my chest with the statement, 'And how's this for your wife'. The ladies spluttered, half choked and I was immediately ejected from the room. I was not to know that Doris Lyndon was a very straight-laced, narrow minded lady and was deeply offended by my vulgarity, which at the time I did not realise would cause so much offence. They left shortly afterwards and Kath gave me a ticking off, explaining that I must never again do anything like that, as it was so very rude and had caused her great embarrassment.

By now two weeks had elapsed and it was decided that I would go to Whitley Bay to spend a week with my Auntie Doris and Uncle Jimmy before returning to High Mousen for a final week. They now lived at Earsdon Road, West Monkseaton in the suburbs of Whitley Bay opposite a pub then called The Grange (now The Hunting Lodge). Here I had mains electricity, running water, hot and cold, and I could listen to the radio; they even had a telephone and I remember the number to this day, Whitley Bay 25698. My aunt and uncle were most kind but I got a bit bored, as there was a busy main road outside and only a small back garden, so I didn't have the space that had been available at Mousen. I was, however, taken shopping, then to the beach and was given a free candyfloss by one of Auntie Doris's ex-customers who owned the stall selling them. One night I was taken to see 'Snow White and the Seven Dwarves' at the cinema down the road but was scared witless by the wicked witch. I liked it when my cousin Ian, their son, came home from work as he was building a live steam locomotive in the garage which he fired up for me one night.

After a week Kath and Eric returned to take me back to High Mousen for the final week, which I spent meandering around as before, enjoying the space and solitude of the Northumbrian countryside which I have loved ever since. Before I went home there was a terrible row between Kath and Eric. Whilst Eric was at work, Kath was looking for something and had searched Eric's jacket which was hung on the back of the living room door. When he returned from work he realised what had happened and was furious as he had forbidden Kath ever to look in his pockets – why, I never found out but that was the only time that I ever saw him lose his temper.

I remember the car journey home, arriving back to delighted

parents and to my sister who I hardly recognised as she had grown in the comparatively short time that I had been away. There was still a bit of holiday left so one day I got my bike out and rode to see my friend Philip Bowker who lived in Stodday Village, just over two miles away on the country lanes close to the Lune Estuary, which in those days saw virtually no traffic. He was in and we had a great afternoon but when I arrived home, my mother had been very worried and said that she was not happy about me cycling that distance and not to go again. I often did but she never found out!

It was soon time for me to return to school and move up to Form 2A, which was taught by a small man called Arthur Briggs. There was a little rhyme about him that the kids at school had made up and it went like this: *Mr Briggs, he had some pigs, he kept them down the cellar, one went oink, the others went oink, they all went oink together.* Mr Briggs, however, was a strict teacher who used to shout a lot, had very high standards and was scrupulously fair. During the war he had served as a Petty Officer in the Royal Navy and taken an emergency teachers' training course after he was de-mobbed. He did indeed run a tight ship and all of the kids were scared stiff about going into his class but after we got used to his regime we would have gone to hell and back for him, so much was he loved and respected. It turned out that he and our previous teacher Miss Towler were engaged and were shortly to be married. Our classroom and hers were separated only by a wooden partition with glass windows high up. The partition could be slid open to make one very large room but was always kept closed and locked from both sides, so that two separate classrooms could be used independently. There was a certain amount of competition between the classes on various activities as, despite being engaged, these two teachers were always competing to be better than the other. On one occasion the school was raising money for charity and Mr Briggs was determined to beat Miss Towler. He somehow found out how much money her class had raised and seconds before the deadline, had deposited our money with the headmaster adding sixpence (in old money) to exceed her total. He had obviously boosted our total out of his own pocket to beat her and waited for the repercussions. They came shortly afterwards when she attempted to come into our classroom. Mr Briggs was ready for this and had placed several of the bigger boys behind the door to block it from opening. Miss Towler was furious and demanded that the boys move and let her in but Mr Briggs was adamant that they stay put and keep her out. She disappeared but seconds later her face appeared high up at a partition window at the front of our classroom. She must have been standing on one of the desks and was shouting 'I'll get my own back on you, Briggs, for cheating, just you wait'. By now the kids of both classes were screaming with laughter and although these two teachers were tough, we did have our lighter moments, as they were both good sports. We were now having examinations at the end of each term, which in those days were set by the teachers. They were difficult and although I was never bottom of the class, I was never top either which was exactly as predicted would happen by Miss Fort, who had taught me earlier in the school.

My circle of friends was beginning to widen but I still spent a lot of time with my original friends, David Rack and Judith Hodgson. David and I would often go into town together to spend our pocket money and to check out the second hand shops as even at this tender age, David was mad keen on antiques and second hand bargains. Judith had several cousins who used to visit and a couple of them were boys of a similar age to me. Her cousin Brian I had known since the age of two years old when we started Sunday School together, so when he came we all got on very well together. I continued to enjoy watching Judith's television set as we still had not got one and the programmes were improving and becoming more plentiful. Christmas was different this year as by now, for the first time, I knew of the myth of Father

Christmas but had to go along with it for the sake of my younger sister.

I was also now old enough to stay up late on New Year's Eve and to participate in the rituals performed by my father. It was nice to do things together as he was now working as a bus driver for Lancaster City Transport and worked so much overtime that I hardly ever saw him.

1956

Quite a lot of things happened this year, some which changed my life forever. Early in the year the Sunny Smiles booklets were distributed again at school and Harry Corbett was returning for the gala night at the Ashton Hall, Lancaster. I was determined not to suffer the disappointment I had endured last year and persuaded my parents to let me go on my own. It was a horrible wet night and I arrived two hours early to be first in the queue. When I arrived I was indeed first there and got myself huddled into the doorway to try and keep dry. After about fifteen minutes a black car drew up and a man got out, approached me and as he did so, I realised that it was Harry Corbett. He asked me what I was doing standing in the doorway and my reply was 'Waiting to see you'. He suggested that I might like to wait with him in his car, as it was warmer and dryer than outside. Normally I would not have entertained getting into a car with a stranger but this was not a stranger, he was my hero and I knew him – after all I had seen him plenty of times on other people's television sets. We chatted about all sorts of things and eventually he told me to come with him to see if we could gain access to the hall. He found a side door which was open and as we went inside a town hall official came to greet him and tried to get rid of me. Harry Corbett insisted that I stay and he told the official that I was with him. He went up on the stage to inspect the layout and I was invited up onto the stage with him. He was quite an accomplished pianist and played the piano for me and when he had finished asked me if I played. I told him that I could not, except for the tune of 'Robin Hood' which I played for him with one finger. He said that he would have to go now to get ready and prepare for his performance but before leaving he gave me a photograph of himself with Sooty and Sweep and wrote 'To Reggie' on it. He asked where I would like to sit and said that I could have a seat anywhere in the hall. I chose a balcony seat right at the end overlooking the stage with an absolutely clear view and before he left, he made sure that I was safely installed there. I waited patiently as the hall started filling up and eventually the evening started with various other events, speeches and the presentation of the Sunny Smiles money collected by the various schools. Harry Corbett then started his performance, which we all enjoyed. At the very end of his act, Sooty the glove puppet whispered into his ear and Harry Corbett said, 'You want to play a tune that you have just learned tonight?' Sooty nodded and Harry Corbett said, 'What's it called?' Sooty whispered in his ear again. 'Robin Hood, well go on then,' said Harry Corbett and Sooty with one finger played Robin Hood on the piano. Harry Corbett then looked straight at me in the balcony and gave me a big wave then bowed to the audience and left as his performance was now over.

I rushed home to tell my parents what a wonderful time that I had experienced and proudly showed them the photograph that Harry Corbett had given me with my name written on it by him. They were obviously pleased at my delight and surprised that a famous celebrity had taken such a lot of trouble to make a young boy so happy. After that night I was always a keen fan of Harry Corbett and Sooty right up to the death of Harry Corbett and still have a soft spot for Sooty despite him having a new master.

One or two of my school friends had joined the Lads' Club on Dallas Road. One had to be ten years old to join but I think that they were trying to attract more members and were letting boys join who were going to be ten on their next birthday. I used to go along some evenings to play billiards and darts. One could also do football, running and boxing but I was not really a sporty sort so only participated in these more energetic activities occasionally.

During the summer there was a large fundraising event which attracted a huge amount of people. Frankie Vaughan, a famous entertainer of the time, had been evacuated to Lancaster as a boy and had enjoyed membership of the Lads' Club and still took an interest in it. He organised several well-known celebrities along with himself to come and sign autographs at a Fete being held one summer afternoon. It was a blisteringly hot day and I had a great time winning several prizes and some money on the various stalls. I was not usually so lucky but on that day, I could do nothing wrong so had a wonderful time.

Every summer an old wartime friend of my mum's used to come to visit us. She was called Miss Kenna and lived in London but came to stay in Lancaster for a few days every year and always came to tea with us on one of her free afternoons. Before she left she always gave Marilyn and I a Half Crown each, which then was like a king's ransom to me representing about five weeks' pocket money. I don't quite remember what happened that year but I was locked out in the back yard for misbehaving in her presence. I remember being furious and shouting to be let back in but no one took any notice of me. I soon cured that by picking up a stone and throwing it through the window showering Miss Kenna in broken glass. I was given the customary damn good thrashing and put to bed and didn't get my Half Crown until quite some time later.

Kath and Eric came again to stay and I really hoped that I would get invited back with them again. No such luck this time and I was bitterly disappointed when they went home and I did not go with them, but later on in the summer I found out why. My dad had bought a car, old even by 1956 standards – it was a 1934 Hillman with the registration number FS9963. My mum named it 'Fussy' as it had the letters FS and was very fussy as to whether or not it wanted to function. Kath and Eric had invited us all to stay at Mousen, so late in the summer off we all went to Northumberland. My dad was not sure where off the A1 road the lane was to the house, as in those days it was not signposted but as we got there I proudly showed him the way and we all arrived safely. I don't think that my parents were very impressed as even by our humble expectations, they found the lack of facilities very inconvenient. We did not stay long and after a couple of days went to Whitley Bay to stay with my dad's brother, my Uncle Archie, and his wife my Aunt Dora, who my dad hated. Around the corner lived the widow of my dad's uncle, my Aunt Laura, and my dad decided that we should all pop round to visit her. Aunt Dora pointed out to my dad that she was not even a blood relative of his and going to see her was an unnecessary fuss. My dad then came out with the phrase, which came into our family folklore, 'There are blood relations and bloody relations and you know what you are'. I seem to remember that we did not stay long after that and on the way home the car broke down at Barnard Castle so we eventually got home at about three o'clock in the morning. Following that, there were many parental rows and eventually the car was sold.

After the summer holidays it was time to go back to school to my new class 3A under the supervision of my new teacher Sid D'Alton. He was an Irishman with a silly Irish sense of humour and an affable personality but I did not seem to learn much during that year. After the high standard that Arthur Briggs had got us to, I suppose any teacher had his work cut out to follow that standard.

For years, I had badly wanted a camera and at last on my tenth birthday, my wish was granted. My dad gave me his old Ensign Full Vue camera and I was delighted. He had loaded it with a roll of film but I was warned to use it sparingly as I would have to pay for the processing and for any subsequent rolls of film. I can remember taking my very first picture, which was of Marilyn standing on the corner of Queen Street and Aldcliffe Road. The rest of my tenth birthday I remember nothing about, as this gift of a camera overshadowed everything.

Before long, Christmas was upon us and I was appearing along with a lot of my friends in the Lads' Club pantomime. We were being assisted by the Joan Ward School of Dancing and most of the girls were about fourteen to seventeen years old. They were absolutely gorgeous and I fell in love with them all. I was very small for my age and being one of the youngest, they thought I was cute. I managed to kiss them all almost every night and my friends were most envious but in reality these girls were completely out of my league with such an age and size difference, but what a wonderful time I had during that week attracting so much attention from those beautiful girls.

I had now become much more socially aware of the various visitors who came to see us prior to Christmas. Most were old friends of my mum from her wartime days in Lancaster and they came to bring presents for Marilyn and myself. My mum and dad always purchased a cheap bottle of port and sherry at this time of the year to be able to offer our guests a drink and this was the only time that we had any alcohol in the house as my parents weren't big drinkers and alcohol was relatively expensive.

New Year once again came and went and I cannot remember anything unusual making this one stand out from the rest.

1957

I don't recall precisely when the Partridges left us but after a long wait, they had managed to secure a council house on Mayfield Avenue, Lancaster. My mother and Sylvia Partridge had become very firm friends so we still saw plenty of them although now on a social basis, but it was still necessary to recruit new lodgers. Len and Mary Burch came to live with us along with their young sons, Grant and Christopher. Len was the Labour party agent for the Lancaster Branch of the Labour Party, which often caused heated debates between him and my staunch Conservative parents.

I got on quite well with Len and during school holidays I would go to work with him to help duplicate leaflets, then fold them and put them into envelopes. I would also run errands and was happy to be his general dogsbody, probably saving him a lot of time on the small menial tasks. Some days I would get paid and some days not but I do remember getting the odd two shillings here and there which greatly supplemented my pocket money. Various influential people from the local community would come and go from his office and even at the tender age of ten, I got a flavour of what party politics were all about.

All went reasonably well for a while and occasionally political callers would come to the house. One started coming rather frequently when Len was at work and I realised that Mary Burch was letting him in even when the bell was not being rung. At a time when he often called, I listened outside her door and heard a tap on the window. I rushed and opened the front door to let her guest in and they both looked most uncomfortable. I was too young to realise the full implication of what was obviously was going on but inevitably Mary Burch disappeared one day with the frequent caller and Len was stranded with their children. On that day, I had to babysit whilst my mum and Len went off somewhere to make arrangements and she was in fact very supportive to him until things settled down. Len had influential friends, who, under the circumstances, quickly wangled him a council house on the Ridge Estate; Mary returned so they too now left us. I mention names here as at the time all of this was in the public domain so I am not divulging anything that was confidential.

Miss Kenna was due again for her annual visit and after the fiasco of the previous year, my mother was determined that I should create a good impression. During lunchtime she did role play with me, she was Miss Kenna and I had to walk through the door, shake her hand and greet her. This was practised several times until I was word perfect. When I arrived back from school, Miss Kenna was sitting in her usual chair and I walked up to her, shook her by the hand and said, 'It is so nice to see you again'. Miss Kenna beamed and my mother bristled with pride until Miss Kenna said how beautifully I had done that and I replied, 'Well it should be ok, I've been practising all lunchtime'. Miss Kenna roared and laughed as my mother tried to hide her embarrassment but I still got my Half Crown when she left.

About this time my best friend David Rack moved away from Lancaster as his father had got promotion with his job at National Cash Registers and they went to live in Stoke-on-Trent. They frequently came back to visit as David's granny still lived on Portland Street so I still got to see David during most school holidays.

After the summer holidays it was time to go back to school to my new class 4A. This was the top class in the school and we were all now top dogs. To our astonishment we got Arthur Briggs back again as there had been a re-shuffle of teachers. After Mr Briggs and Miss Towler had got married, one of them had to leave as in those days teachers married to each other could not teach in the same school. So Miss Towler had left and the whole Junior Section of the school was re-structured with Mr D'Alton taking 2A, Mr Gardner 3A and Mr Briggs 4A. We were all so pleased and Mr Briggs seemed pleased to have us, as we all knew what we were getting and there was no breaking-in process.

During the previous year, I had started school dinners so imagine my astonishment one day when I saw my mum standing with all the other dinner ladies waiting to serve our dinners. It turned out that after applying for the job she had received an acceptance that morning asking her to start immediately, so had no chance to warn me until I saw her standing there. For me this was not a good thing as now the teachers had instant access to my mum should they have a problem with me and whilst I was not generally a problematic child, it certainly kept me on my toes.

During the previous year I had joined the Wolf Cubs and earlier this year our pack had competed in the heats for the Annual Cub Sports. Whilst I was not particularly sporty, I had teamed up with another Cub called John Shepherd as we seemed to co-ordinate particularly well together in the three legged race. At the Annual Cub Sports we won the first heat and got into the final but did not quite win, although coming a close second.

Every day my parents used to get the Daily Mirror newspaper; I cannot imagine why as it was a socialist paper and they were staunch Tories. I often used to look at it before I went off to school and one morning got a shock to see John Shepherd's face on the front page. It turned out that he had drowned whilst taking a short cut across a field with a reservoir underneath and had stepped on an unsafe manhole cover, which had collapsed, resulting in him disappearing into the underground reservoir and drowning. It was quite horrible to read this in the paper without prior warning as it was the very first time that a friend of mine had died and I was shocked and upset, especially as only a few months earlier we had raced together, each of us with one of our legs tied to the other's which had created a physical as well as an emotional bond. I thought about nothing else all day and my mind was definitely not on my school work. During the evening my cub leader called at our house to break the news and asked my mother's permission for me to go along with other cubs to form a guard of honour at the cemetery gates for John's funeral, which we did as a final tribute and farewell to our friend.

One day my dad took me to one side and told me that we might be moving to Canada. He explained that there had been a long process to go through and that for several months he had been going through that process. Subject to the whole family passing a medical examination we would be going to live in London, Ontario close to Lake Erie in Canada, which he showed me on a map. I was a little apprehensive about this forthcoming new chapter in my life and leaving behind all of my friends but at the same time excited about the prospect of such a change. In due course our whole family went to Liverpool and we all had to strip off for a collective family medical, myself and my dad in just our underpants and my mum and sister in just their knickers. It felt just a little permissive for that time in my life as I had never seen my mum topless since breastfeeding my sister when I was five years old and I was not very comfortable with the situation. Eventually it was over and we went to a restaurant for a meal, a rare treat for us in those days. A little time later when the results of the medical examination were known, it was found that my mother had thyroid problems and had failed her medical examination, so the move to Canada never happened.

A few weeks after going back to school, probably about October, Kath and Eric arrived with their daughter Susan and their little Shih Tzu dog called Changi. Sue was about a year old and it was the first time that we had met her. It turned out that Kath had had a very bad pregnancy resulting in almost losing Sue. As Sue was not expected to live, the nursing staff had baptised her at birth, which I understand is permissible under such circumstances. I found out afterwards that things were not going well between Kath and Eric and they had come to Lancaster to talk things over with my parents, hoping that a spark of guidance might emerge. Ultimately it did not and not too long afterwards they had split up, with Kath leaving Eric and taking Susan with her. I only caught snatches as to what was going on as my parents were very secretive at the time about all of this and all that I got from my mother was, 'You will understand as you get older'!

As Christmas came round again I became involved in the Lads' Club Pantomime once again and looked forward to the return of the Joan Ward Dancing Girls. No such luck this year as we got the Mary Woodhouse School of Dancing. The girls were much closer to our age and looked at us as if we had just crawled out from beneath a stone. They wanted absolutely nothing to do with us and offstage were snobbish, and if we tried to be friendly, just gave us black looks and walked away.

The Christmas and New Year festivities came and went and soon we were starting yet another year.

1958

At school this was our most important year, as we were now in the final weeks before our 11+ examinations. This was a selection process to decide which pupils were suitable for a Grammar School education. We were being intensively coached on a number of subjects but particularly English and maths. Mr Gardner was brought in to try out his invention of maths bingo, which consisted of a two part test. Firstly we were handed out bingo cards but standard numbers were not called out. Instead two numbers multiplied by each other were called so that you had to mentally calculate the answer then cover the number on the card if it was there. Half way through the lesson the cards were changed so that the numbers multiplied by each other were on each square of the bingo card and plain numbers were called out. Each winner was given a threepenny bit so the competition was intense; we learned quickly and the school invariably got the money back as the winnings were usually spent in the school tuck shop. Whilst this was undoubtedly bribery and corruption, everyone was a winner. Every day there were five new words chalked on the blackboard when we started class. We had to look up each word in the dictionary and write it and its meaning five times, which meant twenty five lines of writing before we started our school day. Mr Briggs concentrated very hard on teaching us decimals, fractions and areas of all shapes including triangles. He also taught us about circumferences, diameters and areas of circles. He drummed into us every conceivable short cut in mental arithmetic and had a reputation amongst all of the secondary schools, that any pupil who had been through his class was good at maths.

His other passions were football, cricket and swimming. Sadly I was not good at any of these things and despite his trying, he never succeeded at turning me into a fast mover. In my class, however, were some talented lads and with Mr Briggs's tuition, our school won every sporting trophy that they competed for in 1958.

One first that I did achieve, however, was peeing over the top of the toilet wall. The only urinal for the boys was a large stone cubicle outside in the playground without a roof. For years we had always tried to pee over the top of the toilet wall and, to the great hilarity of my friends, one day I achieved this feat and was the first to do so. The competition increased and the following week another member of my class achieved this dubious feat but with disastrous consequences. Arthur Briggs was standing on the other side of the wall and soon realised that on a fine sunny day, it could not be raining. He soon put two and two together, stormed into the toilets and caught the culprit. Once back in the classroom the boys all got a stern warning that any boy caught peeing over the top of the toilet wall again would be sent to the headmaster to be caned. My parents had always wanted me to be the best in the class at something, perhaps English, maths or some sporting event, but would have been mortified if they had found out that I was champion pee-er being the first to scale the toilet wall. They never did find out that in this one thing, I was top of the class.

We were a very large class with 49 pupils, which was the largest number allowed per teacher at that time. One day we had an extra pupil which made 50 and Mr Briggs was terrified that he would be found out if there was an on the spot inspection. He explained the situation to us and we all promised that we would lie should an inspector ask us any questions and insist that our class had never exceeded the regulation 49 pupils.

Throughout my Junior School life a merit badge was awarded weekly in the school assembly to one person in each class for any sort of exceptional achievement. I had never come near to receiving this honour until now and one week I was first equal with another class member. Two badges were never awarded so it would always automatically go to the pupil who had never ever received one in the past. With our class being the top class, we always had to wait until last for the recipient's name to be called. I proudly waited for this award to be bestowed and to my horror it went to my rival who had frequently been awarded it in the past. My bitter disappointment was beyond description and I was absolutely bereft. When I got back to class, Arthur Briggs just had to see the look on my face to realise that I was seriously upset and suddenly the penny dropped. He had made a catastrophic clerical error, inadvertently cheating me out of this entitlement and could see how much that it had meant to me. He apologised profusely and publicly in front of the whole class and sympathised but explained that now that the award had been made, nothing could be changed. I had ranted on at home all week of how I was going to win this badge and on the preceding day before the assembly, how I would be coming home with this honour and now felt so humiliated when I arrived home without it. My parents were very sympathetic and even to this day, I put it down as one of the most disappointing experiences of my life.

We eventually took our 11+ examinations and if I remember correctly, 22 pupils passed for the Grammar School with 2 borderline cases of which I was one. This meant that I had to re-take the examination the following year but as it was age handicapped, borderline cases rarely passed and because of the age disadvantage, had I been a few months younger, I probably would have scraped through the examination first time round. This was a triumph for Arthur Briggs as he had a larger pass rate than any other Lancaster school and he was delighted. My parents had promised me the reward of a one pound note if I passed and nothing if I failed but being a borderline case put them in a quandary. Although I had not passed, neither had I failed so eventually they compromised and gave me a ten shilling note – the most money that I had ever possessed in my life.

After we had taken our examinations there was very little else to do so Arthur Briggs busied himself teaching us about life, politics, job hunting and culture. He introduced us to classical music played on a wind up gramophone and related to us some of his experiences in the navy and how during his travels he had come across other cultures in the world. He taught us about life, values and how to approach the adult world that awaited us; I have always been forever grateful to that man who equipped myself and my classmates for our lives ahead.

Before we left Dallas Road School we went on the school trip to Chester Zoo and the weather was dreadful, being cold and wet. The previous year we had been to the Lake District, which had been even colder and wetter. In those days an outing to Chester Zoo in the rain was not to be recommended and I recall it being a miserable experience as there were not many indoor places that one could go in to keep dry. One of the few places under cover, however, was the young elephant house where small elephants were just behind a tubular metal barrier. I stopped to stroke one of the elephants whilst my friend John Miller walked past ignoring them. Suddenly a trunk came out from behind him and gave him an almighty whack across his bottom with such force that he broke into an involuntary sprint then fell flat on his face. I roared with laughter and fortunately only his pride was injured. On the way there we had driven through Preston and seen Tom Finney, a famous professional footballer of the day, just sitting on the steps of his place of work. At that point the weather had been still dry and all of the kids were thrilled to see this famous personality.

All too soon it was time to break up for the summer holidays and leave Dallas Road School forever. One little girl, Zoe Hodgson, who had cried because she was scared of Mr Briggs when starting in Class 2A, now wept and wept because she did not want to leave him and that was the feeling of myself and most of my classmates. The final day was spent autographing things for friends and saying goodbye in the knowledge that some of them I might never see again. I remember it being a lovely hot summer's day, which went quickly, all too quickly.

During the summer holidays we did not go anywhere but I did go off to Morecambe quite a lot with my friend David Rack as he was spending the holidays with his granny, Mrs Teale, a delightful old lady who I loved. She often took David and me to Morecambe and whilst he and I played, she would sit in the sun and usually chat to anyone and everyone nearby. We often went off combing the beach for glass pop bottles, which in those days carried a deposit when returned. We would identify the outlets that sold the various brands as shown on the labels, cash in the bottles and with the proceeds go across the road to the amusement arcades and gamble our money away. We would also purchase seafood, sweets and pop from the stalls by the beach depending on how successful that we had been on the day. In the meantime David's granny would still be chatting to all who would listen and we had no adult supervision whatsoever whilst enjoying ourselves spending our proceeds. I'm sure that it was illegal to be in the amusement arcades at the age of eleven without an adult but we never misbehaved, although we did sometimes get thrown out if too successful winning more money than we were spending on the machines. We certainly were never short of money on our days out in Morecambe owing to our ingenuity and cunning. Wet days would be spent in our gang hut, an area in the external rear of Mrs Teale's house designed to store refuse bins. It had a secure door and bins were never put into there so we acquired a small table and two chairs, installed them and used to sit in there for hours reading American comics by candlelight. We weren't normally allowed candles or matches but in our gang hut, no one interfered with us and we never got found out. David's mum and dad always stayed a day or two before they took him home, so often I was taken out for a picnic with them all. We occasionally ended up at Cleveleys but I was not keen on that destination, as there never seemed to be any pop bottles and they parked the car as far away as possible from the amusement arcades. I now know why!

During this time my friend Judith Hodgson and I used to walk up to Aldcliffe Village, about a mile away from where we lived, to see one of Judith's friends called Janet Steele. Next to the village was a very large derelict house in its own grounds called Aldcliffe Hall. It was possible to gain access to this house through an external cellar door and one or two other places, so we often used to play in there. Some of the rooms were not safe because of rotting flooring but Janet knew all of the safe places and warned us of the rooms to avoid. We also had to avoid a man who frequently came to check the premises and several times he tried to catch us but we always managed to evade him and escape. Janet explained that he was surveying the very overgrown and extensive grounds for graves of the family who had occupied the hall in the past. She and all of the local people knew of their location but would not tell any outsiders as once the graves had been located and the bodies were exhumed and moved, building work could start. Janet showed me the graves, well hidden by years of undergrowth and I gave my word that I would never tell anyone where they were and never did. Eventually the graves were found and the site was indeed developed and houses built.

At last September came and it was time to start at my new school,

Ripley Boys' School, on Ashton Road, Lancaster, which was about a fifteen minute walk from Portland Street. My mum had tried for the Friends' School, which was a private school but when she realised that she could not afford the top up fees, it was Ripley that became the choice. It had an excellent reputation so this seemed to be the best place to go. Sadly they were so wrong, a new headmaster had been appointed and under his guidance the school had quickly descended in its quality to being one of the worst schools in town for academic teaching and discipline. It did, however, have wonderful facilities for a school of that time with a separate gymnasium, a sports field, an athletics track, its own produce garden and was a large and imposing building. It was a Church of England School which had its own chapel, complete with a superb pipe organ.

The first day on my way to school, I bumped into my friend Eric Rogerson who had been through most of Dallas Road School with me and was also going to Ripley. Eric was even smaller than me and was sporting a brand new school uniform, which absolutely swamped him. My parents could not afford the uniform and my mother was adamant that she would not buy it for another two years in case I passed the examination to go to the Technical School which was taken two years later. I had a smart, presentable light brown suit which had been passed down to me from Judith Hodgson's cousin called Peter Thompson, whose mother worked in a local department store that only sold the best quality clothes. I did not mind the hand me downs as they always looked like new and were of excellent quality and I was old enough to begin to understand the financial struggle that my mother had to constantly wrestle with. I did, however, always have new shoes when necessary and had been bought a pair to start my new school.

Eric and I quickly walked up the Ashton Road and into the school playground, which was much bigger than the one that we had been used to at our old school and full of so many older and larger boys. We both felt a little lost until a second year boy came up to us called Alf Coward who offered to show us the ropes and took us under his wing. For a boy of that age he was very kind and explained how he had felt when he had started school here the year before. I have always remained friends with Alf right to the present day and have never forgotten what a wonderful and generous character that he is and always has been.

The structure here was quite different to what we had been used to. At Junior School our class teacher taught us most of our lessons; here one had to move around the school between each lesson as each teacher had their own specialist subject to teach. We did, however, have a form teacher called Mr Irving nicknamed 'Archie' which I am sure was not his real name and English was his subject. He had a dry sense of humour which was demonstrated when a misbehaving boy had a book thrown at him by Archie and was told to read out the title aloud. 'There's no escape' read the boy and Archie said 'Remember that', with a wry grin on his face. Looking back now he strikes me as a man who probably spent more time than he should have done down at the pub and who can blame him after a day's teaching at Ripley! The classes were streamed into A, B and C classes and Eric and I were both in 1A. I cannot remember the numbers of pupils in each class but it was certainly fewer than Junior School, probably about 35 pupils to a class.

During our first days at Ripley, I spent playtimes wandering around the perimeter of the school grounds barely comprehending how immense it was compared to what I had been used to and soon found my way around. The school itself was also large but after a few weeks, I got used to that too. We now had P.E. in the gymnasium and did sports on the sports field next to it. Our sports teacher was called Alan Duckles but most pupils substituted the first letter of his surname for one two letters further up the alphabet and that is what he was irreverently called by many. I was not one of them as I did not and still don't, use four letter words or obscene language. I am not a prude and probably my silent vocabulary of these words is greater than those who do use them but I don't do it. On occasions I can find these words amusing in certain contexts but I still choose not to use them and if they have to be explained I will partially spell them with middle letters missing so that the recipient is perfectly aware of what I mean without demeaning myself by actually saying them. During my first few weeks at Ripley School my vocabulary was greatly expanded – not by the teachers but by the elder boys using all of the words which I have chosen not to use either then or now.

I found most lessons quite easy owing to the excellent standard that Arthur Briggs had got us to and much of the work I had already covered in junior school. In our first examinations I was ninth in the class, which sounds good but considering that I had learnt hardly anything and that others had beaten me, I should have been ashamed of myself, as I was capable of doing so much better. This was now to set the trend for my whole school life, to do just enough work to keep out of trouble and enjoy myself as much as possible. One subject which I did excel at during my life at Ripley was algebra. We had never ventured into that territory with Arthur Briggs and the subject fascinated me. Owing to the high mathematical standard that Arthur Briggs had taken us to, I quickly picked up the concept of algebra and in that subject, I was top of the class. This I had achieved in my Christmas exams and now that they were over, we were allowed a week of fun and games. We brought all sorts of things to school and during that time I learnt to play Monopoly, Chess and a few card games. I was now widening my circle of friends and during the Christmas holidays, visits were made between our various houses to compare the booty that we had each received for Christmas.

It was about now that our family at last rented our first television set. My mum and dad decided that they could afford a second hand one on rental from Rediffusion. I have no idea how much it cost them but it must have been at a reasonable price otherwise we would not have had it. I think that there were just two channels by now, BBC and ITV, and of course in those days there was no colour television available.

At New Year I was now allowed a small glass of wine to let the New Year in with my parents and felt more adult with being able to join in the festivities, taking a responsible drink at this one and only time of the year when it was offered.

1959

Early in the year my life was again blighted by the death of a second close friend called Derek Crompton who lived on Regent Street in the Ambulance Station, as his father was the Ambulance Superintendent. They had rather a nice garden with a decent sized lawn on which we played cricket during the summer months. Derek once told me that he had an elder brother called Neville who had died at the age of four years old of silent pneumonia. I saw Derek the day before he died as I was passing his house and we said 'Hello' to each other. He was running as if in a hurry to get home as it was lunchtime and he was probably late for his dinner. By the following evening he was dead having also succumbed to silent pneumonia. Again I was terribly upset having lost two different friends at the tender age of only twelve years old – I was quickly learning that nothing in life is certain and to take nothing for granted. It must have been a terrible blow for Derek's parents having lost two young sons and a great worry for the welfare of their one remaining child, Derek's sister Audrey, who did thankfully survive and who I was in touch with until about 1995. Derek and his family had originally come from Manchester and his body was taken back there to be buried with his brother and I remember watching out of the school window from which I could see the railway, viewing the Manchester train going past that was carrying Derek's body and again had great difficulty thinking about anything else that day. Derek's father hardly worked again afterwards and I watched him steadily go downhill until he became a shadow of his former self and eventually died having wasted away. Exactly the same thing had happened with John Shepherd's father who, after John's death, never worked again and eventually died of a broken heart.

I was now really settling down to secondary school life and the routine that went with it. As I have said earlier, I was not good at games but one thing Ripley School did excel at, was producing very good cross-country runners. The first time that I ever went out was a complete disaster as after about a mile, I, along with a few others, discovered the new experience of getting a stitch, a terrible cramp-like pain in the abdomen, which feels like it is going to burst. This stopped me in my tracks and despite much encouragement from the teacher running with us, I could hardly move and slowly hobbled back to school. Before going out for a second time the following week, the teacher gave us all a talk on how to overcome this problem. That was despite the intense pain, to keep running and we were assured that the pain would suddenly disappear. As dubious as I was about this advice and the intense pain that I suffered again at approximately the same point, I carried on with determination and miraculously the pain did go. I was now a cross-country runner and although never the best in the class, started to enjoy this activity. As spring progressed we tried sprinting, hurdling and other activities on the athletic track. We also played football, rugby and eventually cricket but I was no good at any of them so never got into any school teams for sporting activity.

Lessons continued to be easy and I continued to freewheel along. I was still not learning anything new in many subjects and in others such as history and geography, which were quite different to junior school, I did learn just enough to keep the teachers happy. We also did woodwork, which I liked, taught by an affable man called Ken Baines. We never, however, really did enough work to challenge us, so I found some of the lessons boring. This was a shame as I am sure that had the structure been different, I and others would have done so much better. Science lessons were fun and were actually quite interesting. The teacher was called Mr Jones and must have been nearing retirement but he did make the lessons entertaining and I did learn quite a lot from him.

We were never taught by our headmaster, a short man with glasses called J. R. Daykin. I never did find out what the JR stood for but because these were his initials, his nickname was 'Jam rag', the slang expression for a sanitary towel. I was just beginning to find out about such things and most other matters sexual. Most of the older boys talked about little else and this was a whole new world opening up to us, the world of the adult, what men and women did but never talked about and because of that, made us more curious than ever what it was all about. In the school library was the complete set of the 'Encyclopaedia Britannica', so we looked up 'Reproduction' and sure enough we found what we needed to know with illustrations but not very meaningful, being of side elevation and sliced. I did know what girls looked like as I had seen plenty of their bits whilst at Junior School – it was quite amazing how many had been prepared to expose themselves albeit briefly – but I had never known why they were different to boys... now I did.

Our biology lessons were taught by a lady called Mrs Simpson and during spring many of them were spent in the school garden. We cleared the ground ready for growing a large variety of vegetables such as peas, beans, potatoes, beetroot and lettuce. Towards the end of the summer term we could purchase these to take home at a very reasonable price and my mother was delighted with the price and quality of the produce.

Just before our school holidays there was a school trip to the Isle of Man for which my parents paid. I think that this was because they could not afford to let me go on the school holiday to Blankenberge in Belgium earlier in the year so this was the compromise. The weather was good and we had about three hours to explore Douglas without supervision but were told to be back in good time to catch the return ferry, which would not wait for us. One incentive to behave was that the Isle of Man had the punishment of birching for youngsters who got into the hands of the police, so our behaviour there was impeccable despite there being no adult supervision.

When summer holidays eventually came along my mother received a letter from David Rack's mother inviting me to go and spend a week with them at Stoke-on-Trent. I was delighted to receive this invitation and it was arranged for my mother to put me on the bus at Lancaster and Mrs Rack with David to meet me at Newcastle-under-Lyme. This was the first time that I had travelled such a distance alone and in the days before motorways, it probably took about three hours. When the bus reached Newcastle, sure enough the Racks were there to meet me and we caught another bus to the suburb of Stoke-on-Trent called Weston Coyney, which was where they lived.

The road on which they lived was called Horton Drive and was right on the edge of the hamlet next to a sandstone quarry. David knew his way around this quarry and took me for my exploratory visit to see everything that it might have to offer for a twelve year old boy. Eventually we came upon the dynamite store, which was a substantial pebble-dashed brick building with a stout green door secured by a hefty padlock. We got higher up in the quarry and started throwing large stones at the building in the hopes that it might blow up but gave up after a while when we realised that our efforts were futile. After tea we watched television until bedtime, a great novelty for me, as the programmes were different from those at home. We both slept in the front bedroom in David's parents' double bed whilst his parents slept in the back bedroom. We took a while to get to sleep, probably because of the novelty of the situation.

The next day was bright and sunny and after breakfast, David took me to the local shop down the road and showed me around more of the area. I cannot remember what happened during the afternoon but during the evening we went on our own on the bus to see the motorcycle speedway. When we got there David saw some girls that he was at school with and one of them had a father who was an official at the track. She took us up into an elevated box where we had a much better view of the speedway and spent the evening with them watching the motorcyclists compete. Before we left the girls invited us round to their house to listen to records and a couple of days later we found ourselves there and had an enjoyable afternoon. David warned me not to mention to his mum that we had been invited out by girls but that we had been invited by school friends because if she thought it was girls who had invited us, we may have been prevented from going.

During my time there we also went to the cinema, fished at Longton Park and shopped in Hanley. In the evenings we watched a lot of television and on one evening played a simple form of golf out in the Racks' back garden where they had put a hole in the lawn for such purposes. On my very last day there, David's granny came to stay, the same Lancaster granny who lived opposite me in Portland Street. She had been staying with David's Aunty Marion and Uncle Bob in Stockport and it was easier to drop her off in Weston Coyney than go all the way back to Lancaster, then Mr Rack could drive both her and me back the following day. The sleeping arrangements were interesting with Mr and Mrs Rack returning to their own bed, David and his granny sharing a bed in the back bedroom and me sleeping on the floor in the back bedroom on David's side of the bed. David and

I hatched up a plan that when the lights were all off: I would make scratching noises like a mouse, which we thought would be fun. This I did and Mrs Teale shot up in bed and wanted to disturb David's parents thinking that there was a mouse around. I pretended to be asleep and eventually David settled her down and all was back in darkness when I repeated the process. David by now was getting worried and picked up a book from the bedside cabinet and hit me hard over the head with it to make me stop, which I did.

Once the school holidays were over I was back at school, no longer a new boy in this strange and larger world but a more experienced pupil and moving up to Class 2A. We had been given a talk suggesting that we might watch out for new pupils and help them to overcome the strangeness of their new school by showing them round and being kind to them and now realised why Alf Coward had been so good to us the previous year. I cannot remember spotting anyone in distress, so do not recall any acts of kindness handed out by myself to the younger pupils. The daily routine of school soon set in but before long it was my thirteenth birthday and I got the amazing present of an airgun. I suspect it was as much for my dad's benefit as it was for mine but I was very pleased with it. We did a lot of target practice down in our cellar using pellets and darts and put the targets on an old back gate propped up against the wall. I had a party and several of my new friends from school came. Soon we were down in the cellar seeing who was the best shot, when all of the electricity went off. It turned out that someone had shot a dart straight into the main cable coming out of the electric meter and had blown a fuse. My mother freaked out and ordered everyone upstairs where they all piled onto the settee. With the weight of many adolescent boys, two legs of the settee gave way so that the settee was standing at a strange angle. We immediately had tea, then my mother threw everyone out vowing that I would never have another party and nor would Marilyn after she reached secondary school age.

One of my great pals at that time was a boy called Graham Larkin who had a large mop of red hair and was a great motor enthusiast as well as having an amazing knowledge of guns and bombs for a twelve year old boy. He also had a rude sense of humour, as did we all at that age, and out of earshot of our parents the language was pretty strong except from myself for reasons explained earlier. I sometimes went round to his house immediately after school as he lived very close to Ripley School and as his parents were at work, he had a key. One day he was standing on a chair to access a high kitchen cupboard when he put his hand on the very top to support himself and found himself clutching a paperback book. He looked at the title and found that it was a manual on sex and when he read the contents his eyes almost popped out. The next evening he had a large audience of boys all clamouring to read this sexually explicit book and he always replaced it back where he had found it, so that access was available for quite some time afterwards.

In the fields of the Bowerham area of Lancaster was an army shooting range, where the conscript soldiers had to do their target practice. In the evenings we used to go there and unearth the spent bullet brass casings that had not been collected by the army and acquired a large collection of these, which had come from various rifles and machine guns. Occasionally we would find a live round, which had been dropped accidently and Graham eventually collected quite a lot of these. He meticulously pulled out the bullet heads and emptied the cordite from inside the casings into a small container that he kept on the rear room windowsill next to his dad's pipe which was only smoked occasionally. After he first did this Mr Larkin decided one day to have a smoke, filled his pipe with tobacco, lit it and settled down in his chair for a peaceful smoke, there was suddenly a great whoosh and all of the hot tobacco blew out of his pipe as he shot up in his chair, batting out all of the burning debris. He immediately realised that some of the cordite had somehow found its way into his pipe, them being in close proximity to each other and Graham got into pretty serious trouble.

I didn't go much to the Lads' Club anymore but was persuaded by Eric Rogerson to join the Boys' Brigade affiliated to St. Thomas's Church in Lancaster. I had already been in the Life Boys and the Wolf Cubs when I was younger so was quite used to these sorts of organisations. Usually an attendance at Church Parade was obligatory but as I was a regular attender at The Prestbyterian Chuch Sunday School that counted so I never went to church parade. The Boys' Brigade had a drum and bugle band and after a while I was asked to join it. Band practice was on a Tuesday night run by the father of a fellow member of our company, so after much tuition I eventually played the bugle. We were meant to keep practising at home but my mother would not allow it as our dog 'Rip' would start howling every time I started to play.

I had long outgrown my little bike that I had first had and for a while I was without one but it was about this time, probably Christmas this year that my parents found me another second hand bike more suited to my increased size. As I was still rather small for my age, I seem to remember that the bicycle was on the big side but it lasted me for another couple of years as I grew into it. I recall it being a bit old fashioned and heavy but it got me around as I was now often visiting my many friends who lived in various parts of Lancaster.

Being in the second year at school, I had auditioned and been picked for the school choir along with a few fellow classmates. As our school had its own chapel, each one of us had our own specific pew and for special services we were robed in a cassock and surplice. Every week we had choir practice and occasionally during school hours we would have to go and sing elsewhere which suited me, as it got us out of lessons. I did, however, enjoy singing with the choir in the school chapel accompanied by its wonderful pipe organ played by a very gifted boy called Paul Baxter who was about two years older than me. The Christmas carol service was absolutely superb and we had practised especially for the occasion 'Stille Nacht, Heilige Nacht', which is the original German version of the carol 'Silent Night'. I was told by everyone that it sounded just like a German Choir and created a real Christmas atmosphere.

I don't recall specifically our New Year celebrations of 1960 but feel sure that they would have been the same as usual and feel a little guilty of not taking more notice as we were now into a new decade.

1960

In many respects this year was to be one of the turning points in my life. During the beginning of the year everything went along as usual at school but in other respects I was starting to grow up and was turning into a teenager. One of the things that I had usually done for several years was to attend the Saturday morning pictures when the Odeon Cinema put on a special programme of films for children during term time at school. The entire show lasted for only about an hour and a half but we did enjoy some excellent children's films and a serial. Discipline was enforced by a team of volunteer children called 'The Committee'. A good friend of mine had got himself onto the committee and now being thirteen years old, he like most of us was taking an interest in girls. I recall that he had taken a special interest in a particularly well developed girl and vowed that he was going to sit next to her and see far he could get in fondling her breasts. The next Saturday morning there were several of his mates including myself sitting in the row behind him and sure enough after the big film had started so did he. The young lady concerned did not flinch as his hand caressed her forbidden territory and the audience of his friends behind watched in awe and envy as his hands explored and stroked the upper part of her young body. She did in fact become his girlfriend for quite a while until they both got older and moved on.

As the year moved into springtime it was time for us to take the entrance examination to assess our suitability for the Technical School. Every year there was an intake of twenty eight boys and twenty eight girls covering the whole of the Lancaster and Morecambe area, which included the Lune Valley and villages south of Lancaster as far as Garstang. I knew that this was going to be very tough but had decided that I wanted to leave Ripley School so I worked very hard for once in my life to try and ensure a place at the 'Tech' as this was my last real opportunity to improve my chances. When the results came through, I was delighted to find that I had passed and I was now really going to a superb school where I would have a chance to better myself.

Ripley School this year was organising a school holiday to Ireland and staying in a school camp in a small town called Skerries. It had been possible since school had started in September the previous year to bring a small amount of money to school each week and as the holiday was not until July after the school had broken up, it equated to about forty instalments. This made each instalment very affordable; I therefore was allowed to go. I had also been lucky enough to go on the school trip again to the Isle of Man, sailing from Fleetwood. The day was beautiful, the crossings were calm and when I got there, I teamed up with a classmate called Gordon Langley and we went round Douglas together arriving back in good time to catch the ferry home.

Because I knew that I was leaving Ripley, I probably worked even less hard than I had done before and my heart was not into anything except leaving school. Before I left there was a school leavers' service in the chapel and after that you walked away for ever. I did not quite do that, however, as I had the holiday in Ireland to look forward to.

We were taking the ferry from Holyhead to Dun Laoghaire but in order to get to Holyhead, we collectively caught the train from

Lancaster, a steam train in those days. At Holyhead we boarded the ferry to Ireland and were left unsupervised until we reached our destination. I have always been an excellent traveller but my mother being concerned that I might be seasick had made me promise to take some travel pills called 'Quells' before we sailed. This I did and before long I was flat out and fast asleep; the next thing that I knew was being woken up by two complete strangers who told me that the ferry had docked. They had been concerned that I was not stirring and might be left behind and indeed I nearly was. I was still very drowsy and took a while to come round whilst still trying to locate the rest of my school party, which eventually I did. I realised what the cause of this must have been and despite my promise did not take another pill on the return journey and was perfectly fine.

The school camp at Skerries were blocks of wooden huts painted light blue with a recreational grass patch in the middle of the site and the whole area was surrounded by a perimeter fence. In appearance it closely resembled a prisoner of war camp like you see in war films and this was endorsed by the flippant remarks by a teacher when he first saw it. One of the huts was decked out like a café-cum-coffee bar with a juke box and pinball machine where we could entertain ourselves. We were also allowed to leave the camp and explore the town but were told only to go in pairs or groups, as there might be some hostility from local people, us being English in the Republic of Ireland. Nothing, however, could have been further from the truth as the locals were delightful, friendly, helpful and really lovely people with whom we got on very well.

The week that we were there was some sort of special week with the fair being in town. There were lots of stalls, many of which involved some sort of gambling and would not have been allowed in England but the stallholders seemed very relaxed about us enjoying ourselves and sometimes having quite good wins. The local girls of our age were pretty, good fun and we had none of the problems that we might have had at home kissing the girls. It was all innocent teenage fun and that is really just as far as it went. Soon it was time to go home and after I walked away from my friends on Lancaster Castle Station, then I really had left Ripley and it was time to start my new life at the Tech. I cannot remember how many of us went from Ripley to the Technical School. Eric Rogerson was one and I also remember a boy called Albert Kelsall being another. For some reason Albert's nickname was 'Willie', so I did have at least two friends going with me. On the first day I also discovered a good friend from my Dallas Road school days called Wesley Oakes. 'Wes' as we called him had moved into the senior school at Dallas Road and like ourselves had passed the entrance examination for the Tech, so I immediately had three friends in the same class as myself. For the first time in my life, I had a brand new school uniform, which consisted of a maroon blazer, grey trousers and a school cap. It transpired that it was the custom of the older boys to initiate the starters by pulling the button out of the centre of their caps which was called 'Debuttonising'. When I realised that there was no alternative, I carefully removed my own button so that the cap did not get ripped. My mother, however, was not impressed when I arrived home with her hard earned money having been spent on clothing which I had deliberately defaced.

As schools go the Tech was very small with a total pupil population of about one hundred and thirty scholars split roughly into about half boys and half girls. The classes were not mixed as the girls had an entirely different syllabus to the boys but the whole school shared the same playground so that recreation time was mixed. We had assembly every morning which was also mixed but as there were prayers and hymns, the Roman Catholic teachers and pupils had their religious element in a separate classroom and rejoined the whole school for notices and any non-religious activities that came at the latter part of the assembly. The classes were again split into years, the first year boys being T1, the second year T2 and the third year T3. The situation with the girls' classes was similar but I cannot remember what their classes were called. There was common academic ground for boys and girls in lessons like English, history, geography, art, religious education and chemistry. In physics, however, I think that the boys were taught to a higher level and the boys also did woodwork, metalwork and practical drawing which were not taught to the girls at all. The girls, however, did a small amount of domestic science as well as a lot of commerce, shorthand and typing, which the boys never came into contact with. We were being trained to go into industry and had been selected for having reasonable academic skills but with the aptitude and potential to back those up with practical ability as in those days no one envisaged how computers would change all of our lives.

Our teachers were a very mixed bunch of people led by our headmaster called Harold Kay, nicknamed 'Killer'. He was a no nonsense man but firm and fair and had reputedly gained his reputation for once knocking out a boy who had attacked him. No one ever challenged him as he had let it be known that during his time in the Royal Air Force, probably in the 1940s, he had been an undefeated boxing champion. He was not afraid to use the cane and for small matters of discipline would always do it publicly in front of the whole class but for major transgressions, the caning took place at the end of assembly in front of the whole school. Girls were never caned, however, and I really do not know what happened to them as punishment for their misdemeanours but whatever it was, it certainly was not in front of the whole school.

We also did games once a week, usually on a Friday morning. When I first started at the Tech we did mainly cross-country running which suited me as I had already done plenty of that and with the exception of my two classmates who had moved with me from Ripley, no one else had done that sport. For the first time in my life, I found a sporting event at which I was better than anyone else and was way in front. From the directions that we had been given, we had to cross a stream. I was so far ahead that I had time to move all of the stepping stones behind me as I went forward, so that I was the only one running with dry feet and finished well ahead of the others. I don't think that anyone realised that there were originally any stepping stones there so I got away with it. We also sometimes played football on a field called Quay Meadow and I remember one particularly wet morning, I got so soaked that my shorts became semi-transparent. As we never wore underpants under our shorts, little was left to the imagination and I had to walk the half mile or so back to school with my football shirt firmly held down with both hands on the outside of my shorts so as not to be arrested for indecent exposure, much to the amusement of my classmates. I complained to my parents when I got home and received a new pair of shorts made of a more substantial material in time for the next games lesson.

I had recently acquired from a family friend, the gift of a dummy hand grenade which he had kept when being demobilised from doing his national service in the army. A dummy grenade was painted white to distinguish it from the real thing and was drilled to prevent it from being put back into use but in every other way it was real. One day I was foolish enough to take it to school and during an English lesson was transferring it from my case into a desk when the teacher demanded that I bring whatever I had in my hand to her desk and return to mine. I duly walked up to the front of the class and placed the grenade on her desk in front of a sniggering class but a stunned teacher and walked back to my desk. I was immediately called back and asked what the object was, replying that it was a hand grenade. I was then asked if it was live and replied that it was not and was quite safe but the teacher looked unconvinced. I proceeded to dismantle it and explain how it worked, proving that there was no detonator and it was incapable of being filled with explosive. It was handed back to me with the threat of confiscation should I ever bring it to school again.

Despite having moved to a new school, I still kept in touch with some of my school friends that I had met at Ripley, particularly Graham Larkin, and sometimes after school and usually at weekends we would spend time at each other's houses. Graham had purchased a motorbike which he was renovating and would be allowed to ride after he was sixteen years of age and he taught me a lot about engines whilst I helped him as his labourer. I also used to still spend a little time with Judith Hodgson at both of our houses. We had grown up together and despite her being a girl, she was a good friend and not at this point my girlfriend. Many of my male friends thought it rather odd that I should enjoy the company of a girl without romantic attachment but Judith and I had known each other for so long we were almost like brother and sister enjoying similar interests and each other's company.

My father's Aunt Laura from Whitley Bay used to come and stay with us every year and had done since I was a baby. She always came in the autumn and stayed for about two weeks. As very few people then had telephones, she used to write about twice a week to her daughter-in-law, Mary Smaile who lived in Haltwhistle, Northumberland. Mary's husband Reg was my dad's cousin and they had one daughter the same age as me called Rosalind. One day I heard the postman come and my mother picking up the mail then taking a letter upstairs to Aunt Laura who was having a late lie-in in bed. About two minutes later I heard a terrible wail followed by Aunt Laura crying and shouting 'Mary, Mary'. My mother shot back upstairs to see what the problem was and the letter had been sent by her son Reg, telling her that Mary had died from an accidental overdose of her prescribed medication. It turned out that Mary had taken her dose before going to bed and got up in the night an hour or two later probably forgetting that she had already taken her medication and took it all over again. By the following morning she was dead. Aunt Laura could not settle and insisted on travelling to Haltwhistle to stay and see what she could do to help – which was probably not very much at the age of 83 years old – so my father borrowed a car and took her to stay with Reg and Rosalind.

Christmas that year was spent at home and flitting around amongst various friends and entertaining them when they visited us. On December 27th I started work as a paper boy delivering early morning and evening papers for Norman Bell on King Street. I earned ten shillings a week which was more money than I had ever had regularly in my life but not a lot for the unsocial hours that I put in mornings and evenings, amounting to about two hours a day, six days a week. Sundays were a separate entity and done by an entirely different team of people. My first paper round covered Middle Street, High Street, Dallas Road, Blades Street and Castle Hill but was soon modified to King Street, Queen Street, Dallas Road and Blades Street, which had a heavier load than the original round.

I cannot remember anything specific about New Year but that would have been the usual family rituals.

1961

Although I did not know it yet this was going to be a very memorable year in my life. I was beginning to grow up now and things were beginning to happen to me that I did not understand. Just before the February break at school, I had asked a girl in the same year as me at the Tech if I could take her to the cinema and she agreed. There were a few of us going but before that she had invited me to her house one morning for a coffee. She lived at Heysham, so I caught the bus and when I arrived she was babysitting for two younger siblings who kept out of the way. She made me a coffee and we chatted for about half an hour before I left, agreeing to meet a day or two later for the cinema date. The day came when she, myself and our friends occupied the back seat of the cinema and I sat with my arm around her. As the film wore on we kissed several times and I realised that I was seriously in love, I was overwhelmed and besotted by this lovely girl and would have died for her. The time went all too quickly and it was time for us to part. I could not wait for school to start so I popped over to Heysham to see her again but she was out. There was another sibling close to her age looking after three or four others who said they would tell her that I had called.

School started the following week and I could not wait to see her but when I did, she looked a little upset, handed me a note and said not to ask any questions. The note basically said that she could not see me again and towards the end, the writing had become less and less distinct as if she was upset when writing it and ended with the words, 'I'm sorry but it cannot be helped'. Looking back now I think I know the reasons why this so quickly came to an end but at the time I was heartbroken and could not understand why everything had gone so horribly wrong. I had kissed the girl and she had responded, I had not touched her inappropriately and always had treated her with total respect. I think that when I had been invited to the house, she knew that her parents would be out and that the two siblings were sworn to secrecy. My undoing was going back to the house when more of the family were there and she would have had to explain herself to her parents, who then found out what was going on. Her name was Catharine and she was a Roman Catholic Anglo-Indian girl. Coming from that culture, her parents must have freaked out when they realised that she had been entertaining a white non-Catholic boy and I am now sure that she was made to write the letter and forbidden to have anything more to do with me, especially as we were both only fourteen years of age. In those days there was more parental control than there is now in all cultures but particularly in hers and she would have not dared to disobey them. This was my first love, I was growing up and at that moment did not like it very much.

I am told that afterwards, I was very moody and my schoolwork certainly suffered as I came to terms with emotions that I had never experienced before. No one had or probably could explain to me that this is what happens to teenagers and the differences that take place inside are just as profound as those that take place on the outside and one just has to grow through the experience and hopefully emerge from the other side as a well-rounded adult, but I was a long way from that and, who knows? Maybe I still am!

My parents had heard from Aunt Laura who had asked if she could come and stay for Easter. She arrived by car driven by Harold her son who lived near London as after a spell staying in Haltwhistle she had gone to him and his wife Ethel for a while. Aunt Laura and Ethel hated each other, hence the letter to my parents asking if she could have a break with us before going back to Haltwhistle. After a few days my mother realised that all was not well and called the doctor to examine her and the verdict was Senile Decay, which we now call Senile Dementia. My parents got in touch with her son Reg in Haltwhistle and my father borrowed a car to return her to stay with him. That sadly was not for long as she continued to deteriorate and only about a month later died at the age of 84 years old.

A little time went on and my mother was beginning to have health problems. Firstly she felt ill and then noticed an abdominal swelling so went to the doctor who did the preliminary diagnosis of an ovarian cyst. Several tests were done and eventually she was told that she was pregnant. I could not believe it, I was fourteen years old, none of my friends' mums were pregnant and I was going to have a little brother or sister fifteen years younger than myself and I was very embarrassed. It came as a complete shock that my mother and father were still having sex, as at the age of fourteen, one thinks of parents in their forties and fifties as having one foot in the grave and therefore being incapable of such acts!

Several friends of mine smoked and I soon also got hooked and used to join the smokers group, hiding at school for a cigarette during the break. My parents found out and said that they preferred that I did it openly, so I used to smoke at home. I was able to afford the cigarettes as my paper round money easily paid for this addiction and ten shillings a week went a long way in those days. When my friend David Rack came to stay next time I discovered that he was also now smoking, and as his granny smoked we used to sit in her house and all have a cigarette together but he dare not do it in front of his parents as they had forbidden him to smoke. On one occasion David's dad almost caught us but his granny covered up for us saying that only she was smoking, despite the room resembling the great London smogs of the 1950s.

At school it was now late spring and the heats were being held for the school sports. It was compulsory to enter for two events unless one was entering for the mile race and for this event, owing to its tiring nature, you were exempted from having to do another. I entered for the 100 yard and 440 yard races knowing that on the first, I would not stand a chance and on the second, I could not win but would not come last and in the event of things that is exactly what happened. I was now out of the school sports, which suited me fine and was chatting to friends when I was told to be quiet by a teacher. Shortly afterwards I forgot myself and started chatting again. 'Stoddon,' he shouted, 'you are going to do the one mile heat as a punishment for disobeying me.'

'Sir,' I protested, 'I am not allowed to do that as I have already run two heats.' 'Yes I know,' he said, 'but you will do it anyway and that will keep you quiet.'

I boiled with anger and thought that I would show him, so when the heat started I set off pacing the winner until the end and with a final burst won the heat. Endurance was my strength and I did not find the one mile race too much effort but as a consequence found myself in the school sports competing with older and more capable boys, so only came in fourth in the final.

As I have stated before, my paper round covered Blades Street and at that time there was a traditional grocer's shop there called 'Burleys' run by a man called Eddie Burley with his wife Margaret. They did good trade with the children from Dallas Road School, as a quick nip through a back alley opposite the school got you straight to their shop.

One evening when I was delivering their evening paper, Eddie Burley asked me to wait a minute whilst he finished serving some customers. He then came over to me and asked how much I earned delivering papers and I told him ten shillings a week. 'Come and work for me and I will give you a pound a week,' he said. He explained that I would be expected to turn up shortly after school finished and work until five thirty all weekdays except Wednesdays when the shop was closed because of half day opening. I would also be expected to work on Saturday morning from nine o'clock until twelve thirty. This was two and a half hours a week less than my paper round and I did not have to get up early in the morning. I immediately said yes and was told to start the following week. I made my way back to Norman Bell's paper shop and told him that I would be finishing at the end of the week as I had got a better job. He asked how much I was going to be paid and when I told him, a look of disbelief spread across his face. He had a reputation for being mean and I had been poached!

The following Monday I started and immediately liked Eddie and Margaret. Eddie was an affable, soft-hearted man and Margaret was gruff and stern, at least on the outside. I soon realised that she had to appear like this as many customers would try and take advantage of her in delaying paying bills so she had to be firm. In reality she was hard on the outside and soft on the inside and when I got to know her, I would have gone to the ends of the earth for her, as she was so good, fair and considerate to me. Eddie was not always in the shop owing to the fact that he also had the job as a bus conductor on the Ribble Buses. How he managed to do that I will never know, as he was a cripple with one leg that would not work properly which he dragged around. On the double deck buses he would hop from step to step at great speed to get upstairs and down, his bad leg somehow following him. It became obvious to me that they did not always find life easy and despite having the shop and Eddie working, money was tight. They had two young daughters, Janice and Alison; Janice was very like her mum and Alison like her dad.

I was provided with a large and heavy grocer's bicycle with a huge deep basket on the front, which was used to deliver orders and collect stock. Most evenings I was given about thirty pounds and sent to the wholesalers to collect various items including cigarettes. The wholesalers were on Moor Lane and called W.R and H. Riley. It was in a dingy, untidy shop run by a grumpy bald headed man called Horace Riley. His son Ken occasionally helped him and was considerably more cheerful and helpful. Every Friday I had to go to the Lunesdale Farmers' warehouse on Water Street to collect ten dozen eggs, which were two dozen to a tray and stacked five trays high. The stacked trays were put into a large cardboard box, which I then lowered into the basket on the front of the bike. The biggest problem was getting out of Water Street into the rush hour traffic which in those days, before Lancaster's one way system, was the junction where all of the traffic converged. Water Street then was a cul-de-sac and was the only street on the junction without a traffic light, so breaking out into the main stream of traffic on my grocer's bike was a nightmare. One evening there was a policeman manually changing the traffic lights from a control box situated at the junction. There was always about a one second delay with all of the lights being at red before one direction changed to green and the only way of exiting Water Street on my well-loaded bicycle was during this short delay. When the time came, I shot across the road and the policeman jumped out in front of me, stopped me and told me to wait. When he had got the traffic flowing he came across and accused me of jumping the red light and said that I would be reported. I was not in the habit of arguing with the police but insisted that I was completely innocent as Water Street was not controlled by the system and indeed did not even have a traffic light, endorsing my argument by stating that if it had one, I would have been happy to obey it. The policeman looked across the road, realised that I was right and sent me on my way, telling me that he would let me off this time but if it happened again, I would be in trouble. The same thing did happen again every week, as it was the only way that I could get into the system but fortunately I never saw that policeman again.

When I was out and about on the bicycle, I always left the shop back gate unbolted and off the latch so when I returned I could ride up to it and tap it open with the basket holder on the front of the bike and the gate would fly open. One evening I did this but the gate had been locked by Janice and Alison, who were sat on the top step at the back door of the shop awaiting my return. The gate being locked did not give and the whole assembly of the gate and gateposts crashed down into the yard as the delighted little girls shouted 'Timber' and ran off. I was horrified and had to go and confess to Margaret what had happened and offered to pay for the damage. She was quite relaxed about it and said that everything had needed replacing for some time as the woodwork was rotten and I was not to worry about it.

Saturday morning was when I had to work hard and fast, making up orders and then delivering them. The worst delivery was to an address on Castle Park which was not far away but up a big hill. I could never pedal the fully laden bike up the hill so I used to ride to the railway station and push the bike up a footpath to Castle Park, which was a short cut. Riding back was no problem as it was mainly downhill and with an empty basket. Next, I always had to go to a customer on Dale Street called Mrs Heggerty. She had originally lived on Blades Street, but still kept her account with the Burleys and got an enormous grocery order, which I had to deliver every Saturday morning. Dale Street was about half a mile from Blades Street and up a succession of hills so I was always panting when I got there. One Saturday morning I knocked and knocked on her door but could not get a reply although I knew that someone was in as I could hear noises from inside the house. Eventually a midwife in a dark blue dress answered the door and angrily asked what I wanted. I explained that I had the grocery order to drop off but she was having none of it and refused to accept the delivery despite my fruitless attempts to give it to her, told me to go away and return at twelve o'clock. Two hours later I had the return journey with the puffing and panting to do all over again but this time when the same midwife opened the door, she was in a better frame of mind and informed me that Mrs Heggerty was now safely delivered of her new baby and that my first attempts of delivery had coincided with Mrs Heggerty's.

Early September, I started back at school and found that a couple of my classmates like me were interested in photography and did their own developing and printing. One of them, Bill Holden, invited me to his house one Saturday morning where he showed me how to make contact prints in the darkroom and told me where to get the paper and chemicals. I could not afford to buy a contact printing frame so I made one out of hardboard, glass and masking tape held together by a bulldog clip. I purchased the chemicals from Vince & Co in Cheapside and used some old bowls donated by my mum in which to develop my paper. I did this in the cellar at night when it was dark using a safelight given to me by a family friend, I dug out a lot of my dad's old negatives and in no time at all I was making photographs. I was absolutely thrilled with the results and was surprised how easy that it was to do. I was now completely hooked on photography. My birthday was nearing so I asked for a better camera and it came in the shape of a Bencini Comet, a 127 camera sold exclusively by Boots. This was still only a basic camera but was a lot better than my Ensign Full Vue as it was capable of taking a flashgun, which I purchased soon afterwards. I also purchased some developing dishes which now also allowed me to develop my films, albeit in total darkness and leaving as much chemical solution on the floor and over me as was left in the dish but it did not matter: I now felt like a real photographer.

I had now saved a little money and during the school holidays wanted to go and stay in Northumberland. Eddie and Margaret gave me a few days off and I went to stay with my Auntie Doris, having written to her a few days earlier to ask if I could go. In those days there was a daily bus service from Blackpool to Newcastle-on-Tyne run by the Primrose Bus Company so I went on that bus. My Auntie Doris, a widow by now, met me at Newcastle and we caught the train back to West Monkseaton Station which was about 100 yards away from her house on Earsdon Road. Whilst there I visited my Auntie Dora and Uncle Archie in Whitley Bay as well as my cousin Reg who by now had been married several years to his wife Madge and lived in Monkseaton. They had two children, my second cousins, Christine and Kenneth. I also asked my Auntie Doris to take me to visit my cousin's wife Mary whom I had never met. She had been married to George but had tragically been left a widow when George had died unexpectedly the previous year with a brain haemorrhage at the age of thirty nine leaving her with a son, my second cousin Philip. My mother had asked me to convey an invitation for Mary to come and stay in Lancaster for a holiday and to meet our side of the family who at that time she did not know. When I met Mary and told her of my mother's invitation she said that she would consider it and reply to my mother in due course. This she did and arranged to come for a holiday a few months later and on meeting my mother found that they were kindred spirits in many things – including finding fault with all of the Stoddon men! – and remained the very best of friends for the rest of my mother's life.

My mother was now becoming heavily pregnant and suddenly got the taste for cider. We had never had a constant supply of alcohol in the house before and in 1961 the dangers of drinking alcohol during pregnancy was not known or at least not well publicised. During the last three months of her pregnancy, she consumed gallons of the stuff and there was always a couple of bottles in the kitchen. She did not mind us helping ourselves and I can remember one evening drinking two large glasses of this beverage and feeling a little dizzy and slightly sick. This was my first experience of overindulging in alcohol since the brandy incident when I was a two year old.

On Regent Street, adjacent to Portland Street, lived a large family consisting of father, mother and seven children. They were the James family and one of the boys, Harold, along with his brother John had found and dragged an old four seater canoe out of the River Lune. The find had been reported to the police but the canoe had not been claimed so they patched up its leaks and used to sail it on the Lancaster Canal. One evening they invited me along and we had a great time paddling a mile or so to the Lancaster Aqueduct Bridge. On the return journey there were several boys waiting for us, all stood on a bridge called 'Ridge Bridge', as it led to the Ridge Council Estate. As we passed underneath and emerged from the other side they started throwing stones at us as we furiously paddled to get away. I was incensed by their behaviour as we had done nothing to provoke them and was determined that I would try to get my own back on them. A few evenings later, I was invited to go again but this time I went armed with my Milbro Catapult and a bag of stones. Exactly the same thing happened again and when we were just out of their stone throwing range, I got out the catapult, loaded a stone and hit one of them in the chest with the first shot. He let out a yell of pain and they all ran off the bridge and started to chase us down the towpath. We had a good start on them and paddled more furiously than we had done on the previous occasion and eventually lost them. The next time that the James brothers went in that direction, Harold took an airgun but without ammunition, and the very sight of that apparently did the trick and just the action of pointing the airgun at them made them scatter.

At school about this time, Killer Kay came into our classroom one day and said that he would like us all to volunteer for extra engineering workshop practice straight after school on Tuesdays and Thursdays at the College of Further Education about two miles away. The lessons would last from 4.30pm until 6.00pm and would give us considerably more experience than our predecessors had in this subject. He explained that he could not enforce this and it was entirely voluntary but in fairness to the pupils doing this extra work, the ones that didn't would receive at least three hours additional maths homework per week, so everyone signed up. My dilemma was how the Burleys would take this news and thought that my part time job might be in jeopardy. When I explained the situation to them, they were fine about it and said that on Mondays and Fridays I could come straight from school without going home first and work a little later until everything was cleared up. They also asked me to stay behind a little longer on Saturdays as and when was necessary instead of finishing at 12.30pm and to make sure that all of the work was finished before I went home and said that they would still pay me my one pound per week. The money was always a little better anyway as the customers often used to tip me when I delivered their orders. The arrangement worked well and on a Saturday if Eddie was working, I often helped Margaret serve customers in the shop if she was busy and I had finished my jobs, then I stayed on until the shop had gone quiet. Many of the customers in those days were Irish and lodging on Blades Street. Most of them were the men building the Lancaster section of the M6 motorway that was under construction at that time and sometimes their families had come to live with them as the project took about two years to complete.

I had now started taking my camera and flashgun to school and begun to take candid pictures when the teachers were not present or clandestine ones when they were. My friends were quite amused with the results and I had now started processing all of the photos myself with my rudimentary darkroom setup. I was getting the reputation of the unofficial class photographer and my friend Wes Oakes asked me to come round to his house to photograph his model railway layout! My reputation as a photographer was growing.

One Wednesday night as I was coming home from school, Mrs Teale, my friend David Rack's granny, spotted me and asked me into her house. We sat in front of her fire and both lit a cigarette and she went into her kitchen, returning with a bottle of Martini and two glasses. She handed me a glass, filled it with Martini and then did the same for herself. 'Try this,' she said with a smile on her face, 'it's lovely and I thought that you would like it too.' It turned out that David's Auntie Marion, Mrs Teal's other daughter, had bought it for her but I am sure that Auntie Marion did not envisage her old mum sitting in front of the fire with a fifteen year old boy, sharing her Martini and encouraging a minor to drink and smoke!

On December 6th, my little brother Frederick Scott was born and I was soon allowed to visit him and my mum at the hospital and a few days later they were home. The days of convalescing after leaving hospital were now a thing of the past, so I think that they were home about ten days after the birth. I had now become a bit of a celebrity at school having a new baby brother and just after my mum got home, several classmates asked if they could come back to my house with me to see him, which they did. They all seemed a little envious, several saying that they too would not mind having a little addition to their family.

I worked quite a lot of extra hours at Burleys close to Christmas as the school holidays had started and their shop was busy with customers ordering a lot more food than usual because of Christmas. Christmas Eve was on a Sunday so the Saturday before Christmas was very busy and I seem to remember spending all day at the shop helping until shortly before it closed. As I was leaving, Margaret gave me a five pound note which was a lot of money to me in those days and I refused it. I liked Eddie and Margaret so much and they had been so good to me I expected nothing more than my wages but she insisted that I take it. I was most grateful to them and for the respect and appreciation that they always showed to me and I had not anticipated any extra remuneration.

Nothing momentous happened at Christmas but it was different with a new baby in the house. I cannot remember exactly what I got although it was probably something with a photographic connotation. I do not remember this specific New Year but by now I was allowed to drink a little alcohol in moderation so probably had a beer or two.

At that time it was still legal for a fourteen year old to purchase some types of alcohol from an off licence, so I was able to buy my own booze from the shop in Aldcliffe Place at the bottom of Portland Street who had a selling out licence. At that time the shop was run by Ashton Kenworthy and his family who had taken it over a few years beforehand from a couple of elderly maiden ladies who would never serve a child first whilst an adult was in the shop irrespective of their turn in the queue. Until the Kenworthys took over, children never shopped there as they could be in for a very long wait!

Joy and Lyn Stoddon with Reg (selfie) 1946

Reg and Marilyn c1954

Reg, aged 5

*Reg and Philip Bowker going
fishing at Stodday c1958*

Reg on James' motorbike c1964

1962

This was to be a pivotal year in my life although I did not know it yet, as it started in the same routine way in which most years had started.

After Christmas, I had more money than I had been accustomed to, so at the end of January purchased a second hand Ensign Epsilon 120 rollfilm camera from the sale at G. L. Robertson's Camera shop in Ffrances Passage, Lancaster. This had previously been Vince and Co but they had now moved and changed their name. It cost me thirty shillings and represented a bargain as it had more settings than the previous two cameras I had owned. I was now becoming more enthusiastic and the shop owner, along with his lady assistant, were beginning to recognise me. My father was also a customer there and one day during February, the assistant told him that they were about to advertise for an apprentice to assist Mr Robertson. I was very keen to apply for this and my father conveyed my enthusiasm to the lady assistant. When the advert appeared in the local paper, I applied for the job and went for a short interview with Mr Robertson. He told me that I would be informed whether or not I had been successful after interviewing the seven other people who had applied. A few days later

I was notified that I had been successful and asked me back to arrange when to start.

My father went to see my headmaster Killer Kay at the Technical School who at first was reluctant to release me but when he heard that the job was definite and was an apprenticeship he agreed to let me go. I left school on 2nd March and started work at G. L. Robertson's on 5th March. I walked away from my last day of school without a tear. I had never really liked school, I had never enjoyed schoolwork and the feeling when I walked out of the school gate for the last time was one of elation and total freedom as if a great burden had been lifted from my shoulders. I was really sorry to leave Eddie and Margaret Burley and I did leave them with a tear in my eye as I had grown to love them as if they were part of my family. When my friend and classmate Wes Oakes realised I was leaving, he fancied the job at Burleys and lived only a few doors away on Blades Street, so I put in a good word for him with Eddie and Margaret and he took over from me, starting with them when I started at Robertson's. My school life was now over and it was time to begin my new life as a young working adult.

The start of my working life 1962

My first day at work was a sunny, brisk and cold March Monday morning. It had snowed the previous Friday evening but only a little of the snow settled which had now gone. I arrived at about ten minutes to nine and five minutes later the lady assistant called Lorena Stavert and Mr Robertson both arrived at the same time. The shop was unlocked and the lights switched on and I started my first working day.

The first task was to provide me with a white nylon overall. I was sent with Lorena armed with some petty cash money to Decorous Garments on Dallas Road, Lancaster who made and sold these items. We returned to the shop when I put on this smart new over garment and officially become a member of the staff. Firstly, I was shown around the shop and taught how to work the till. Secondly, I was given a bucket of hot water, a floor cloth and a round tub of 'Ajax', a scouring powder of that day, and told to go and clean the external window surrounds until they were gleaming. This came as a bit of a shock as I did not realise that such menial tasks were part of the agenda and I was afraid that if any of my friends saw me they would find it most amusing. When I had finished I had lots of dusting to do inside the shop and told that when there were no customers to serve this was a continuous task in order to keep the shop and stock looking clean. We were in fact quite busy and I was encouraged to watch what was happening and invited to serve customers when I felt ready to do so. At first I was terrified as most of the customers knew a lot more about photography than me but after about three weeks I plucked up courage and served my first customer.

There were a few initial hitches and particularly one, when an elderly well-spoken lady asked if we still stocked 'Camp'. The only 'Camp' brand name that I knew was a type of chicory liquid coffee substitute so I confidently looked her in the eye and said, 'I'm sorry, madam, but we don't sell coffee.' She scornfully looked back at the spotty fifteen year old and said, 'Young man, I don't mean coffee, I mean corsets.' I was suddenly very embarrassed, felt myself going bright red and not knowing what to say when Mr Robertson came to my rescue explaining to her that the premises that we occupied was no longer the 'Ladies Shop' that she had known, as the proprietor had retired and that we were now a photographic shop. The lady accepted the explanation but still looked unimpressed and she bustled out of the shop muttering to herself. A week or two later I had an equally embarrassing moment when a customer said to me, 'Have you got spots?' I did have: millions of the damn things as I was after all a fifteen year old adolescent, covered in acne and could not understand why a customer should get so personal. I was speechless with embarrassment but once again Mr Robertson came to my rescue, opened a drawer and pulled out a packet of little paper self-adhesive spots that were to be stuck onto the outside of colour slide mounts, so that one could quickly see which way round they had to be inserted into a slide projector. I was quickly learning that there was a little more than I had originally imagined to working in a specialist shop and that I didn't know it all as my youthful cockiness was diminishing.

During the summer Mr Robertson went off on holiday leaving Lorena and me under the watchful eye of a lovely lady called Mrs Gee. She was in fact a locum pharmacist whom Mr Robertson had paid to come in for a week as many of the items that we sold were familiar to her through the pharmaceutical trade. On our second trading day under her wing, a customer came in wanting a demonstration on an Ilford Sportsman camera. Mrs Gee looked a little blank as did Lorena, so I was pushed forward to do the deed. By now I had picked up a little technical knowledge so nervously demonstrated the camera and to my astonishment made the sale. After the customer left we were all jubilant but especially me as it was my very first camera sale and I had proved that I was capable of doing my job, which gave me a huge amount of confidence to sell others in a much more relaxed way, which I am sure gave customers much more confidence in me.

Mr Robertson was very pleased with our performance whilst he had been away and on his return presented me with a Minolta Autocord twin lens reflex camera to use throughout my apprenticeship, to enhance my photographic knowledge and skills. I was absolutely thrilled as this was an expensive camera and cost far more than I could ever have afforded but was the beginning of my very serious photographic endeavours.

At home we had a surprise visitor, Eric Race, who turned up unexpectedly and unannounced. I was delighted to see him but learned later that my parents were not. Eric had always been kind to me and as a young child, I had loved him and enjoyed my stay with him and Kath when I was only eight years old. I was ushered out of the way whilst he and my parents spoke at length but learned later that he had visited them in a last ditch attempt to try and persuade Kath and Sue to return to him after having left a few months earlier. Apparently my parents were unsympathetic as they had never liked Eric but did allow him to stay the night before leaving the next morning. For some reason he had left his car in a car park near Lancaster town centre so when I walked down to work he walked with me, parting when we reached the edge of town. I asked him if I would see him again and he said that he did not know but I urged him to come back some time and he wished me the best of luck in my new job. We shook hands as we parted and I never saw him again. I learned that shortly afterwards Kath had married a wonderful gentleman called David Allen and that he had adopted Sue shortly after the marriage.

As an apprentice I did not earn a lot of money but had managed to save a little and with the help and guidance of my father, had purchased an NSU Quickly 49cc Moped. I had not been able to ride it until my sixteenth birthday but when that day loomed I suddenly had wheels. About a year previously, I had bought a good quality Claud Butler cycle frame from the scrap yard and gradually embellished it with all new parts and wheels but this suddenly took a back seat as my moped gave me much more range with little effort, allowing me to travel far greater distances in a much shorter time.

One day I bumped into my friend from the past, Brian Hodgson, the cousin of Judith who lived close to me. He had just left school and was working on a farm at Barbon, near Kikby Lonsdale, for a couple called Henry and Barbara Martin. It turned out that he had Saturday afternoon and Sunday off every other week so was working every alternate weekend and invited me to go along and give him a hand on the farm on the Sundays that he worked. I accepted the invitation and with my trusty moped went along every other Sunday to help him. Whilst it was completely unpaid, I really enjoyed the work and Barbara Martin always rewarded me with the most splendid farmhouse meal that you could ever imagine at teatime before I returned home. The Martins were in fact a marvellous family, very good to Brian, extremely hard working and kept a superbly run farm. At that point in time they had one child, a baby daughter called Christine, but Barbara seemed to have Christine and the farm work completely under control with the pram containing Christine out in the farmyard, whilst Barbara did her chores.

Lorena Stavert, the girl with whom I was working, got married around this time. She had been engaged to an accountant, John Bell, and decided that she would finish work, as her new home was in Heysham and travelling would be too inconvenient. We were therefore looking for a new young lady who came to us in the shape of Patricia Currie. Pat was the daughter of our new cleaning lady, Mary, who cleaned for both us and the travel agent next door. Mr Robertson had still kept on Mrs Barber (who he nicknamed Ali), our original cleaner, for one day a week but she was getting old and frail and he hadn't the heart to finish her, so let her come in for a couple of hours, until eventually she had to give up through ill health.

Before long Christmas was looming and this year I was looking forward to it as my baby brother was just over a year old and Christmas with a baby is rather special. A week or two beforehand Judith Hodgson popped round and having not seen her for a while, I suddenly realised that she was a pretty young lady and saw her in a more adult way than I had before. Although she lived only around the corner, my mother told me to see her safely home and when we got almost to her door, I put my arms around her and kissed her. She put her arms around me and kissed me back and before I knew it I was very attracted to her and asked her if she would be my girlfriend and she said that she would. When I got back home my mother commented that I had been a while and I made some excuse, as I didn't want her knowing what was going on.

At the shop we were busy for Christmas and the travel agents next door to where I worked invited us to go in and join them upstairs at their party. We could only go one at a time in order to keep our shop open but when my turn arrived, I went upstairs and could hardly believe the amount of food and alcohol available. I had never ever seen so much alcohol in one place at the same time and could have whatever I wanted. I stayed about twenty minutes, had a couple of drinks and when I left the staff there seemed deeply entrenched, getting more and more drunk but were very affable and wonderful company.

During the Christmas and New Year holidays Judith and I were inseparable and I was invited to a big family party that the Hodgson family held every year for their various relatives including Brian, his sister Linda and their parents. I was in my element as I knew most of the family already so felt very at home with everyone. There was good food, alcohol and games. The men played a dice game called crown and anchor and gambled for pennies while the women gossiped and we teenagers were left to amuse ourselves. Judith had invited a school friend to the party, a girl called Carol Lofthouse whom I did not know and little did I know at that point in time that she would be one of my dearest friends later in life; then she was just a shy fourteen year old. We all had a really good time and I was invited to a similar party at Brian's house to do the same all over again. That time soon came and once again I really enjoyed myself as I got along so well with this very sociable family who accepted me as one of their own. After this event, I was invited to yet another party held by Judith and Brian's Uncle Cyril and Auntie Dorothy. I didn't really know them too well but I suppose that I had become a bit of a fixture, being Judith's boyfriend and Brian's friend. Uncle Cyril and Auntie Dorothy had a daughter called Susan and a son called John. I suddenly took a shine to Susan; Judith noticed and asked me to make a choice, Susan or her. I chose Susan, which turned out to be a big mistake as Susan was not in the least bit interested in me so suddenly I had no girlfriend at all.

This is not like me, I don't let people down, I don't lie and I don't cheat and had let Judith down horribly and for no reason. I could not understand myself except to be very ashamed for the upset that I had caused. Brian's mum took me to task, told me off and all I could say was that I was very sorry but could not explain my actions. I suppose it was all of my teenage hormones kicking in and in retrospect I did and do still love Judith but was never in love with her. I had already been in love and knew exactly what that was like, and despite my fondness for Judith, realised that I loved her in the way that I would a sister.

On Boxing Day we had had a little snow and it had become extremely cold so that the slushy snow had now frozen hard on all of the pavements into solid ruts and this was the start of the famous 1962 - 1963 freezing winter that went on for almost three months.

1963

This started off very cold with things everywhere freezing up. At the shop all of the gutters and drainpipes were solid with ice and the River Lune looked like pictures that you see of Alaska with solid ice on both sides and ice floes coming down the river. The sea at Morecambe had chunks of ice floating on top about the size of paving slabs and the beach was full of ice. At home it was bitterly cold as in common with most other people we only had coal fires but no double glazing or any central heating. My father had put a small paraffin lamp behind the toilet and another near to the water tank upstairs to stop them from freezing and every morning when I got up, there was as much ice on the inside of my bedroom window as there was on the outside.

Every other weekend Brian came back from the farm and on the Saturday nights we had started going to the Central Pier at Morecambe where there was dancing. We always went on Brian's motor scooter with me as a pillion passenger. Crash helmets were not obligatory then so I did not wear one and on reaching Morecambe on one occasion found that I could not comb my hair, as it had frozen solid owing to the weather being so cold. I could, however, get an illegal drink as the staff on the Central Pier did not seem too strict so I would regularly have a couple of half pints of beer during the evening. One still had to be careful, however, as even then, the police were strict and impromptu raids were very frequent with them trying to catch under-age drinkers. Brian and I did not have too much luck in attracting the girls on these nights out although we often ended up meeting mutual friends and having a chat and a drink.

As we got well into March the weather at last started to warm up and the great thaw began. By now many underground water mains had frozen with houses here and there having no mains water supply. On Portland Street we were lucky but Pat who worked with me was affected and the water company had turned up to attach some electrical device to thaw out the pipes where she lived, which apparently had worked. There were a lot of bursts but eventually everything got back to normal.

During the really hard spell, I had not been to the farm to help Brian but as the spring got underway I became a regular visitor at Treasonfield Farm to help Brian and the Martins. I had also become friendly with a young man called Martin working for a rival photographic shop and during the week occasionally used to go to his house and we would do darkroom work together making black and white prints. He became involved with a local peace movement which had their headquarters at Langthwaite House, high above Lancaster on the road out to a hamlet called Quernmore. The people who lived there had a permanent open house and were called Paul and Vivien Smoker. They were very much into the Campaign for Nuclear Disarmament movement as were many of the people whom I met through them and although I did not share most of their views, I admired their commitment and liked them. Paul Smoker was a very clever man and was by profession a nuclear scientist so it was very hard to have any sort of discussion on his views as he was so much more expert and knowledgeable than I could ever be – perhaps he was right and I was wrong, or perhaps there is no right or wrong, who knows? During 1963 I spent a lot of time at Langthwaite House, honing my political views and being introduced to people who later would be regarded as hippies. It was a very interesting time but I know that it worried my parents who thought that I might be brainwashed into joining some subversive movement – that wasn't so as these were just very well-meaning people, even if some portions of society regarded them as being misguided and peculiar.

One day in the shop a customer came in, a famous celebrity of the day called Stan Stennett. He was appearing at the Winter Gardens in Morecambe in the Black and White Minstrel Show, which was the stage version of a popular television show of that time. He wanted a photographer to go to a field near Morecambe to take some pictures of him with his son posing alongside his private aeroplane, which he used to commute to and from his home in the south of England to Morecambe. I was allocated this task as I could get to the venue on my moped, so I went along with my camera to take the pictures. All were very successful except the last one where I had to take the aeroplane flying past low as they were leaving. Owing to my inexperience I completely missed the aeroplane and ended up with a blank sky. They were, however, very nice about it and still paid the bill and I was thrilled to have met such a famous person. Little did I know then that over the years, my work would enable me to meet so many more well-known people.

At some point before summer David Rack appeared on the scene to stay with his granny. I don't remember how we met them but one evening we came across two girls, one of whom became my girlfriend and the other one David's. She really drew the short straw as she became besotted with him but not he with her. She always waited until the next time he came to stay and remained faithful to him for about two years. My girlfriend was called Joan and David's was called Susan. I enjoyed Joan's company but was not in love with her and knew that ultimately things would not last – and they didn't. The problem was that I still had not ever got over losing my first love and nothing had been the same since.

At work I was getting very used to serving customers, being given more responsibility and all the while my confidence in what I did was growing. I was constantly coming into contact with our large customer base, which included everyone from people with a very limited budget up to wealthy customers with an unlimited budget. Some of our customers had menial jobs, others were professional people and one was a large employer. He was a man called Thomas Storey who owned several factories in Lancaster employing a total of several thousand people. He was an elderly man in his early eighties of dignified appearance and despite his age was still working. One Monday morning he came into the shop and I served him. He came to leave a film for developing and printing but wanted an assurance that it would be ready to collect on Friday morning of the same week. I gave him the assurance at which point he complained that his previous film had taken longer than the timescale that I had just given him. I explained to him that the service had been improved and assured him that if he called on Friday, his results would be ready to collect. He was still full of doubt and said he would bet me a shilling that his pictures would not be ready on time and I politely accepted his bet. Friday morning came and Mr Robertson went off to the bank; moments later Thomas Storey appeared, presented his ticket and picked up his pictures. He made as if to leave the shop and when he reached the door I said, 'Excuse me, Mr Storey, you bet me a shilling that your pictures would not be ready and they are.' Thomas Storey, without a word, reached into his pocket, pulled out a shilling, slammed it down on the counter and walked out of the shop. About ten minutes later Mr Robertson returned from his visit to the bank with a broad smile on his face, quoting Thomas Storey whom he had met on his return journey and had said to him, 'That cheeky young bugger of yours has just taken a shilling off me'.

The shop was now getting busier than Mr Robertson had envisaged and he decided to look for another sales assistant. I mentioned this to Martin who said that he would be interested so he left our rivals and came to work for us. When we started working together our relationship was not harmonious once we had to spend each and every day in each other's company. He briefly experimented with the drug 'Drinamyl' known then as Purple Hearts and seemed to be more involved with the swinging sixties than me. I know that Mr Robertson became concerned about his activities and used to say 'I don't know what that lad will get up to next'!

A customer of ours, Albert Gillam, invited me to go round to his house to see the darkroom that he had built and the date arranged was for Friday 22nd November. I got home from work just in time to catch a television newsflash that President Kennedy had been shot whilst visiting Dallas in Texas, USA and this came as a terrible shock; he seemed such a capable man, always so full of life. Whilst I was having my tea another newsflash came along to say that he had died from his injuries and the mood at home was most sombre and we all knew that the world suddenly was not quite as safe as it had felt before. After tea I made my way to the bus stop on a cold foggy November night full of gloom and wiping away the odd tear as my eyes were wet with grief. Despite having never met this man, I felt that I knew him as he had occupied so much of the news and was always part of our lives. Whilst I was waiting for the bus to take me to Albert Gillam's house, a total stranger came up to me and said, 'Have you heard about President Kennedy?' I said, 'Yes' and he replied, 'It is a terrible thing'.

The year wore on, Christmas loomed and we became very busy in the shop. Once again we were invited to the party in the travel agent's shop next door and as had happened the previous year there was a large abundance of alcohol. We took turns to go in, with Martin being last as he was the junior assistant. He seemed to stay longer than the rest of us had and eventually returned with one of the travel agent's staff, a girl called Mary. Mary was about two years older than us and was a sturdy, well-endowed farmer's daughter. She and Martin shot upstairs in the shop and about two or three minutes later she came down with a smile on her face followed by Martin looking a little startled and red faced. It turned out that when they had got upstairs Martin had starting kissing Mary and put his hand down her top, fondling her breasts. Mary then plunged her hand down the front of Martin's trousers scoring a direct hit and grabbed him by the testicles, at which point he withdrew his hand from Mary's breasts as the shock of having his testicles squeezed hit him, hence Mary's smile and Martin's red face.

At home Christmas was getting more interesting, having a one year old baby brother to enhance the festive spirit. Judith came round to bring Christmas presents and once again my mother said I had to walk her home. On reaching her house I apologised for what had happened last year and asked if I could start seeing her again. She said 'No', as she had met someone else at her church youth club and did not intend to let him down. I accepted this and wished her well as by now it was obvious there would never be a long term romantic future for us. I did, however, get invited to the series of Hodgsons' Christmas parties once again owing to my continuing friendship with Brian as we were still going to the Central Pier at Morecambe every other Saturday night when he was home from the farm.

1964

As I was now 17 years old this New Year I probably consumed more alcohol than I ever had done before and at some of the Christmas parties had been a bit of an idiot playing practical jokes on people through a drunken haze. In common with most teenagers, I hadn't to come to terms with the greater freedom given to me and the responsibility that goes with it and was still on a learning curve.

At work I was preparing for my preliminary examinations and had been out and about taking photographs to submit and swotting for the practical and written work. Martin, like me, had become an apprentice but was very scornful of the scheme and the training. He regularly used to criticise it, not taking too much interest in the paperwork and reading that was necessary to keep up with the educational side of the work. One of the things that he overlooked was the deadline for submitting the practical work for the first stage of the Preliminary Photographic Dealers' Association Examinations. I decided not to enlighten him and whilst I got on, did my work and sent it off to London, he was blissfully ignorant about his obligations and what was expected of him. The day after the deadline I casually mentioned to Mr Robertson and in Martin's hearing that I had submitted my work and Martin went ballistic accusing me of not telling him. I replied that he had expressed no interest in the scheme or the necessary work and that if he had been diligent in keeping up with his reading, he would have known about what was expected of him. Martin made several hurried and fruitless phone calls to London and eventually realised that he would have to wait a full year to catch up with me. Whilst I was like the cat who got the cream, Martin floundered in frustrated rage. The following week Martin handed in his notice and I was at last rid of him.

In my spare time I was still visiting Brian at work and spending a lot of time at the farm. I had now sold my moped and had purchased an old 98cc James motorbike, having previously passed my motorcycle driving test. Whilst my motorbike was only small it was a lot faster than my moped and had clipped about fifteen minutes off my journey from Lancaster to Barbon when visiting the farm. In 1963 my motorcycle licence also covered driving an agricultural tractor, so I was able to drive the farm tractor on the public road between the fields, and therefore was a much greater help to Henry Martin than I had been before.

I was now getting itchy feet and wanted to go further afield so I decided that in my May holidays I would go to Whitley Bay on my motorbike and stay with my Auntie Doris. My mother was dead against the idea but could not deter me so eventually gave in with a plea that I drive carefully and look after myself. When the time came it was a horrible day and the motorbike had a slow puncture but off I went in the wind and the rain for my first epic journey. The first part was familiar as it took me past the farm at Barbon but after that I was on new territory armed only with an old map borrowed from my dad. I went via Sedbergh, Kirkby Stephen, Brough and onto the A66 to Barnard Castle. In Barnard Castle I stopped for the toilets and then continued on to Bishop Auckland where I stopped to eat my sandwiches and drink my hot coffee from a Thermos flask that I had taken from my rucksack. From there I made my way onto the A1 through Gateshead, over the Tyne Bridge turning left onto Newcastle Quayside where I headed off towards Jesmond Dene by turning left again at the Tyne Tees TV Building. That took me along the Coast Road and on to Whitley Bay. I arrived at my Auntie Doris's house on Earsdon Road six hours later with my face covered in mud thrown up at me by all the lorries passing me on the A1 and Coast Road. At first my Auntie Doris did not recognise me with a muddy face and two eyeholes but eventually I was invited in, got cleaned up and changed into some dry clothes from my rucksack.

I spent a couple of days in Whitley Bay visiting various relatives and going to one of my favourite spots, St Mary's Lighthouse. I especially enjoyed the time spent with my cousin Ian and his wife Eileen as Ian was very much into photography and gadgets so had very similar interests to me. The only difference was that he could afford them and as yet I could not on my low wage as an apprentice. The journey home was much better, the weather being fine and sunny with no rain at all on the way back, which I did in about five hours. My mother was relieved to see me back all in one piece and had worried all the time that I had been away. Not many people had telephones then so I had not been able to contact her to say that I had arrived safely or tell her exactly when I was coming back.

Life at work was very enjoyable without Martin as Pat and I got on very well and enjoyed working for George Robertson who was an easy going and amusing man. He used to occasionally stroke Pat on the bottom if she was bending down but never in the presence of his wife Mary who would have disapproved of such behaviour. During a warm spell I remember a female customer bending down in front of me to put something in her shopping bag. She wore a loose, low cut dress and when she bent down, little was left to the imagination. I have to confess that I did not mind but was a little embarrassed over precisely what to do in such a situation. As usual Mr Robertson was full of worldly wise advice when I mentioned this. He looked at me with a big grin and said, 'If it happens again, have a bloody good look'!

That summer Dave Rack came to visit his granny, arriving from Stoke-on-Trent on his motor scooter. That was great as we both had transport and could get about together, Dave on his scooter and me on my motorbike. After work Dave and I would go for evenings out exploring the area until one night Dave's scooter broke down. Eventually his parents came and he went home with them in their car leaving me with some money and instructions to put his scooter on the train back to Stoke-on-Trent. That proved more complicated that I realised as I had to find the goods department which was an annex of Green Ayre Station, close to the quayside at Lancaster. Fortunately much of the way was downhill so I was able to ride the scooter freewheeling some of the way with only a little pushing necessary here and there. When I arrived I found a school friend of mine working in the office who helped me fill in the paperwork. The office was an antiquated and dingy place covered in a seemingly chaotic sea of paperwork and a big motto on the wall in front of their desks *'If you are in any doubt, send to Preston they'll find out'!* The scooter eventually did arrive at Stoke but I think that David never rode it again but sold it as seen.

At work one day Mr Robertson suggested to me that I go on a two week educational course working with Kodak in London. This would take place in October and he would pay for it if I would pay for my accommodation. There was no way that I could possibly pay for a two week stay in a London hotel as even in those days hotel accommodation was too expensive, so my mother wrote to some of her friends who lived in Brixton and they suggested an old lady called Katie Knights who took in paying guests. My mother wrote to Miss Knights who did have a room and her prices were affordable, so this was arranged. I travelled by overnight coach on Saturday 10th October and my dad came with me to the bus station to see me off. Whilst waiting for the coach, I bumped into an old friend from the Lancaster Lads Club called Ken Ward. Ken was a few years older than me and was working just outside London so we travelled down on the coach together and on arrival at six o'clock in the morning, he showed me where I could get a decent breakfast at a reasonable price opposite, to the side of the New Victoria Cinema. After breakfast we parted and agreed to keep in touch, me giving Ken my telephone number at work and Ken giving me his work number.

I had never been to London before so this was a completely new experience for me. I realised that it was too early to look anyone up so meandered around for an hour or so eventually finding a bus to take me to Brixton. Back in 1964 there was no underground station at Brixton but in any case, I had never used the underground so did not have a clue what to do and would have certainly got lost. It was about ten o'clock in the morning when I arrived at Brixton and it was still a little early so I explored for another hour before calling on my mother's friends. They made me very welcome and took me to Mervan Road to meet Miss Katie Knights with whom I was staying for almost two weeks. She was a lovely, grey haired lady aged about 80 years old. Her house was right out of the Victorian age with black leaded fire grates, heavy dark curtains and Victorian furniture. The whole interior could have come straight out of a museum and it was just like living in the past. In my bedroom there was a washstand and a jug which every morning Miss Knights filled with hot water for me to wash myself. This whole situation was a very interesting and comfortable experience, stepping back in time and living as people had done seventy years ago. It was not like Mousen had been to me as a child, because we did have electricity and the house was always very warm, comforting, clean and tidy. Miss Knights always called me

Mr Stoddon despite the sixty two years age difference between us and I did not have the heart to ask her to call me Reg as I knew that to a person of her generation, that was not the thing to do.

My first meeting with Kodak was at their then headquarters on Kingsway and was scheduled for Monday evening 12th October at six o'clock. There was a reception with snacks and drinks where we were introduced to the staff, given an itinerary for the forthcoming days and shown around the building in which we would work. Work started at 9.00am prompt on Tuesday 13th October when we were all given an assessment test to ascertain the level of photographic knowledge that each of us had. To my astonishment I came out top but that meant that I had to keep working hard to remain at that standard. Each day we finished about five o'clock which meant that if I went straight back to Brixton I got there at about six thirty. I did, however, make several friends, so often at lunchtime, after eating in the Kodak canteen, we popped around the corner to Brewery Lane for a pint of beer in 'The Sugar Loaf' pub. Some evenings I went out with friends exploring London, getting used to the underground and also doing some night photography. Saturday 17th October was a free day but Sunday18th we were taken to a Chinese restaurant for lunch followed by a trip around Regent Park Zoo, then on to the Charing Cross Lyons Corner House where we all had an evening meal. We had all been given a Kodak Retinette Camera plus a movie camera to use for the day and a competition was organised to see who had taken the most amusing photograph – which I did not win or even get placed.

Sunday night at Katie Knights' was a special night when various relatives came to visit and play cards. One was her nephew who brought his daughter, a girl about the same age as me. She was very attractive and I fancied her but there was no point in taking matters any further as I was going home at the end of the week and Katie Knights probably would not have been pleased if I had paid her great niece too much attention. I enjoyed the evening immensely with civilised company and this lovely Victorian atmosphere even down to playing cards on a Sunday night as the Victorians used to do so long ago.

I was slightly late for work the following morning owing to very heavy traffic in Brixton and when I got to the room in which we were working, I found that everyone was waiting for me, all twenty five of them. It turned out that twenty four of them had all been ill during the night, some with diarrhoea, some with vomiting and some with both. They thought that they had narrowed it down to two possibilities from the dishes that we had eaten the previous day, but I had eaten everything and had not been ill so the mystery was never solved. No one went to the pub that lunchtime as everyone was still recovering from a probable dose of food poisoning but as the day progressed so did the health and spirits of my fellow pupils and the Kodak staff. One evening after work a few of us visited St. Paul's Cathedral. It was very quiet with no staff or clergy around and in those days tourism there was not high on the list of their priorities. We wandered around until we found a staircase with a seemingly unending amount of shallow steps which eventually took us up to the whispering gallery. Even on leaving we still saw no one so left to walk back up Ludgate, Fleet Street and the Strand before I caught the bus back to Brixton.

There was now little time left before our course was over and on Thursday 22nd October we had a final assessment examination to see what we had learned. I think that once again I was first but this time equal with two or three others. We finished early that day as we had a gala dinner to attend in the evening where various awards were to be handed out by Mr Len Downing, the head man of the Kodak organisation in the UK. The gala dinner was superb with lots of good food and a continuous flow of alcohol and some drunken singing led and encouraged by our Kodak tutors. I can remember drinking eighteen single whiskies that night along with the wine that we had drunk with our meal. This was the most alcohol that I had ever consumed at one time and although seriously impaired, I was not actually drunk. When it was time to go home several of us caught the underground and at my stop where I had to catch the bus, they bodily threw me off the train and I staggered down the platform, out of the tube into the open air and caught my bus which should have gone to Brixton. We were about two bus stops away from the south side of Vauxhall Bridge when the bus stopped and the conductor announced that the bus was not going any further as their shift had finished and they were out of time. We all had to get off the bus and I started to walk the long road back to Brixton. I must have walked about two miles when I was desperate for a pee. I popped down a back alley to relieve myself and started walking again. I had now got as far as The Oval at Kennington when suddenly I saw a taxi coming in my direction with his sign illuminated. I flagged him down and went the last mile or two back to Mervan Road by taxi which was a great relief as I don't think that I would have quite managed the last part of the journey back on foot.

The next day I was in remarkably good condition and had to be at Kingsway ready for our final event, which was a factory visit to Harrow and then on to Hemel Hempstead to see the film processing works. This was a very interesting and beneficial day seeing how so many things were manufactured and distributed and the large extent of film processing that they undertook at that time. We also went round the Kodak Museum, which in those days was at Harrow and not accessible to the public, so only visitors to the factory could see the museum. We had been taken to the visit by coach but all returned on the train and on our arrival at London dispersed each to make our way home. I went back to Brixton to say goodbye to my mother's friends and then went to Mervan Road to pack my bags, say goodbye to Katie Knights and make my way to Victoria Coach Station for the journey back to Lancaster.

My parents were pleased to see me as the only news of me that they had had was a postcard I had sent to inform them of my safe arrival. A fortnight's mail was also waiting for me and amongst it was a letter from The Footlights Club, an amateur dramatic company that owned The Grand Theatre in Lancaster. Before I left I had written to them expressing my interest in amateur dramatics and asking if I could join their numbers. The reply was favourable and invited me to go and see their membership secretary, Peggy Lamb, who worked in the office of a local radio and television shop, to sign up, pay my membership fee and get details of the meetings.

Back at work I was astonished how much good my Kodak training course had done as my customer approach and sales techniques were much more professional and certainly produced results with a higher volume of successful sales. Mr Robertson was delighted with the new me and I felt so much more confident about what I was doing with the increased level of knowledge that I had acquired. The customers were now often asking to see me, which took some of the burden away from Mr Robertson and I was pleased that, at last, the customers were having confidence in me.

In my spare time I had started going to the Grand Theatre and was making a completely new circle of friends in The Footlights Club. I quickly realised that I was not going to be the best actor in the world but was getting on well with quite a number of young people of a similar age to myself who were working backstage and enjoyed learning that side of the productions. The very first production that I helped with was called 'The Beaux Stratagem' by George Farquhar and I found it quite fascinating to see all of the effort that the audience never see, that goes into presenting a play. I had also been given permission to take photographs on the stage of all the rehearsals with the exception of the full dress rehearsal, so very quickly became the unofficial photographer of The Footlights Club, taking many stage and candid backstage pictures.

The Footlights had a very strong social side with many members retreating to the pub across the road called 'The Shakespeare' after any activities at the Grand Theatre. That was an interesting but basic pub with George, the landlord, who was a good likeness of William Shakespeare. It also had even more basic outside toilets with many rude rhymes and sayings inscribed on the walls by drunken customers. The most amusing one that I remember said, '*My mother made me a homosexual*' and some wit had added underneath, '*If I send her the wool, will she make me one too*'! We would occasionally go for a meal in one of the few restaurants which were around at that time, particularly a new Indian restaurant that had just opened nearby and then was the only one in Lancaster. At the end of each production after we had cleared the stage, called 'Striking the set', a party took place on the stage and everyone involved with that production would be there. A lot of eating and even more drinking went on and by the time that we went home, it would be well after midnight with many of us very merry and slightly the worse for wear.

I had now acquired a different motorbike, a 198cc Sun which was much faster that my old 98cc James and I could get to the farm faster still and often used to go to Stodday village nearby to see my old pal Philip Bowker who had a motor scooter. I had been going there regularly since I was quite a young boy and it took less than five minutes to get there on my motorbike, a big improvement on the days of pedalling when I had eventually got it down to about twelve minutes. Philip had a friend who lived across the road from himself called Glen Jackson and Glen also had a motorbike. We often went out as a group and met up with other motorcyclists in all sorts of different places. Glen was re-building a motorbike in the cellar of the large house in which he lived and we often used to help him although Glen's father used to give us strange looks when we called and I don't think that he approved of us. Philip's mum and dad, however, seemed to like me and I got on with them particularly well, which was fortunate as I spent much of my spare time with them.

The shop was now getting busier than ever and Mr Robertson decided that we needed another assistant so an advertisement was placed in the local paper and our new member of staff, John Talbot, was appointed. John was very tall and keen on photography, quite a serious person and conscientious in his work. We all got along very well together and the customers also seemed to like him. He lived in Bolton-le-Sands with his mother, who was a nursing sister, his father having died some years earlier. John and I became firm friends and used to enjoy a social life together outside of shop hours.

I was approached by the manager of a local cinema as they were looking for a photographer to record their publicity and promotional events but as his budget was very limited he could only pay the cost price of the materials used so we struck a deal. I would do all of his photography and charge him only for the materials used and in return I had an unlimited free pass, valid for two people, to go to the cinema whenever I wanted. My social life was now in overdrive and I was never at home, having so many friends and activities to occupy myself, but I was having a great time and although I periodically went out on the occasional date with various girls, the romantic side of my life was temporarily on hold.

When my friend Brian Hodgson had his alternate weekends not working, he occasionally popped into the shop to arrange what we would do on a Saturday night. He began to be attracted to Pat with whom I worked and asked me whether or not she had a boyfriend and whether I thought she would go out with him. I told him that to the best of my knowledge she did not have a boyfriend and that if wanted to take her out, he had better ask her, which he eventually did and got a favourable response. This now effectively brought Pat into my social life through Brian.

Christmas was a busy affair with lots of parties to attend and at home the festive season was getting interesting, playing with my brother's numerous toys that he had been given. I did not spend New Year at home but at Brian's house as his mum had held a big New Year's party which was a very Scottish affair; she was Glaswegian and certainly knew how to throw a successful Hogmanay event. I had arranged to stay the night, which was just as well owing to the amount of alcohol consumed that evening and I did not arrive home until the following afternoon.

1965

N ot long after the year began, a letter arrived at work inviting a member of staff to attend an educational course with one of our distributors called Johnsons of Hendon. Johnsons were the importers for Voigtländer cameras and the trip was for three days visiting the camera factory at Braunsweig in Germany with the airfare and accommodation paid for by Johnsons. Mr Robertson was not in the least bit interested but I asked him if he would let me go and he agreed. I had never been abroad or flown in an aeroplane before and was very excited at the prospect of this forthcoming visit, which was to take place towards the end of February. The only expense that I had besides my spending money was the return travel to London. Our flight was departing from Heathrow Airport but our party was being transported from the BEA passenger terminal on Cromwell Road in London, to the airport. I arrived the day before and spent one night with Katie Knights, which had been pre-arranged, and had an afternoon in London re-visiting St. Paul's Cathedral and being amazed by all of the building work that was taking place nearby. Only four months earlier when I visited, it had been partially surrounded with bombed out buildings but these had all now been cleared and the place was now one big building site.

The flight was very exciting in a four engine propeller aircraft, which was noisy with some vibration, compared to the more modern comforts of jet travel. We first stopped in Cologne to drop off and pick up passengers then flew on to Hanover where we were met by coach to take us to Braunsweig. On the coach we were introduced to a German representative of the Voigtländer company who told of the various places to keep away from, such as a dubious nightclub called the 'Melodian' and a notorious street called the 'Winkelstrasse' where all the ladies of easy virtue sat semi naked in windows. When we arrived at our hotel we were allocated our rooms, given a meal and a Voigtländer camera to use during our visit, then told to make our way to a local beer cellar for an evening's entertainment. We were given a town plan which showed all of the streets, so everyone made their way to the evening entertainment via a small detour through the Winkelstrasse and sure enough, there were the ladies, some of them lovely young girls parading themselves in windows, advertising their wares. Even at that age I found it terribly sad that these attractive young women were involved with prostitution when surely, with their looks, they could have found more fulfilling employment than being on the streets. The first day visiting the Voigtländer factory was very interesting as camera manufacturing then was very labour intensive with engineers working on lathes and machines stamping out parts before being assembled by hand and boxed for storage. After one month's storage, the cameras were re-tested before being finally packed and sent out for world distribution. After our evening meal at the hotel, we all then went to the Melodian Club which was basically a strip joint with highly inflated drink prices, but at least we had all experienced the places that we had been warned against and our curiosity had been satisfied.

Part of the second day was spent seeing lens production and the rest being given a two hour lecture on the workings of a new computer which then was their pride and joy but by modern standards probably had less computing power than a pocket calculator has now. We were all bored to tears and I had a struggle to stop myself nodding off, as it was warm inside the factory and minus nine degrees Celsius outside with snow still falling. On the last night we were entertained by Voigtländer in a local hotel with a beautiful meal starting with hors d'oeuvres followed by turtle soup, a main meal and a sweet all washed down by a plentiful supply of German wine. The following morning we all met at the factory for the results of a photographic competition, to judge who had taken the best pictures with the cameras that had been loaned to us. My picture got nowhere but the winner was a very humorous picture of a large pot of flowers placed in a gentleman's urinal. Back in 1965 we had never seen single gents' urinals in the UK so the ones in Germany had a good deal of novelty value and even the Germans found this photograph well executed and very funny. We were then given a superb factory lunch before being shipped off back home.

When I returned home, the realisation hit me that there was a big gap in my education as I had not been able to communicate with any non-English speaking people in Germany. When at school, I had never been taught any foreign language and as German was dominant in the photographic trade during the 1960s I decided that I would go to evening classes to learn German, which I started later in the year.

I did not see as much of Brian now as most of his time at home was spent going out with Pat, although I still did periodically pop over to the farm on my days off, which only took me about forty minutes on my Sun motorcycle. My social life was still very busy juggling my interests with the Grand Theatre, the Photographic Society to which I also belonged, along with my cinema photography and going to the cinema, as well as going out with and visiting my now large circle of friends. Many of them were coming into the shop as customers and the shop seemed to be thriving with rarely a quiet moment. I was getting to know Mrs Robertson quite well by now and knowing her better found that she was not the serious person that I had first thought that she was. If Mr Robertson ever came out with anything rude or slightly vulgar she still had that serious side and would say, 'George, not in front of Reg, he is only a child' but when I would usually start laughing and she would retort, 'You should not understand that anyway!'.

I had never had a blind date before, until one day Phil Bowker said that his friend Glen Jackson's girlfriend had fixed up for two of her friends to join us one Sunday afternoon when we used to sometimes race our motorbikes on a quiet country lane. I can't remember how the girls got there but they soon seemed to get bored with all of the male activity involved and with motorcycling in general. We suggested that a trip to Morecambe might be more interesting so each of us took a girl as a pillion passenger and we arrived in Morecambe shortly afterwards and went bowling at the bowling alley. The girl allocated to me was called Barbara and Philip's was called Mary. It soon became apparent that Barbara had taken a strong dislike to me as had Mary to Philip. During the evening we did a swap which proved to be a much more satisfactory arrangement as I got along quite well with Mary and Barbara tolerated Philip, which is more than she did me. At the end of the day we each took our respective girl home and Mary invited me into her house for a coffee which is exactly what we had and all that we had. When we had chatted and drunk our coffee, Mary saw me to the door, I thanked her for her company, gave her a polite goodnight kiss and never saw her again. Barbara, however, and I kept on bumping into each other and still do to this day. With maturing years and the experiences of life we get on very well together now and often stop for a chat but that was never destined to be a romance and I look back on the memory with amusement and the only time that I

117

succumbed to a blind date.

Shortly afterwards, Glen Jackson had completed the build of his new motorbike, which he had put on the road and was testing. Everything had been successful and he had gone off on a trip for a few days but had never arrived at his destination so was missing. I cannot remember exactly how far he had gone but he was found lying in a ditch unconscious, with a serious stomach injury and his motorbike lying beside him. It appears that he had a few spanners in his front pocket to tweak any minor adjustments that he needed to make, when the engine suddenly seized up, throwing him off the machine with the spanners stabbing him in the stomach as he landed. Unfortunately he and his motorbike ended up in a ditch mostly out of sight from the road and it was only by chance that he was found by a passing motorist who caught sight of something just sticking up from the edge of the road. He was not expected to live but after several months made a slow recovery but was not completely well until about two years later. Not long before that we had lost another friend who had been killed in a motorcycling accident, crashing into a tree at speed whilst taking a bend on the A6 road just outside the small town of Garstang. These events concentrated my mind as to the dangers as well as the joys of motorcycling and at last I was becoming more worldly wise about driving more sensibly.

During the previous two years, my mum had been looking after a boy about two years younger than myself during the school holidays called Bill Shand. She was paid to do this as his mother and father were working and it was a way for my mother to make a little extra money, whilst having to be at home to look after my younger brother Fred. Bill's mother came to see my mother and explained that she would have to be away from home for a few months and could Bill stay and become part of our family during that time? My mother agreed, so for about six months Bill lived with us as if he were part of our family.

The only problem was that sleeping arrangements had to be shuffled around, so my sister got my bedroom and I got her bigger room along with Bill, which we had to share. As my sister had a double bed we both had to share that as well but the arrangement worked and for a few months that is what happened.

Towards the end of June, I got a phone call at the shop from Brian asking if I could go over to the farm at Barbon to help with haymaking as they had a lot of hay to get in and needed to work fast in case the weather broke. I said that this would be ok and rushed over on my motorbike, arriving about seven o'clock. I had never been haymaking before and it was hard manual work, pitchforking each bale of hay onto a trailer. Initially I could not get the hang of doing this and on my first attempt ended up falling over but after a bit of practice realised that it was not brute strength but a knack of flicking the bales up that worked. It was wonderful working in the fields during the long June evenings and although by the end of it I was physically exhausted, I felt fresh and elated mentally as it was so good to work hard without any mental stress attached. On the last night we finished at about nine o'clock and Barbara Martin had prepared what seemed like a banquet for us. On that night I had got a lift over with Brian's parents, so I could drink the beer that Henry Martin had got from the pub to go with this wonderful spread, to celebrate getting all of the hay in before the weather turned and in thanks for the help that we had given.

I managed to arrange a week's holiday in August to coincide with Brian's holiday as he had suggested that we go to Glasgow on his scooter. Just before we set off I got a speck in my eye which I could not easily remove but thought that it would eventually come out of its own accord. Unfortunately it didn't and by the time that we had reached Lockerbie my eye was streaming and the pain unbearable. We stopped at Lockerbie, found the house of a doctor and knocked at the door, which was answered by a boy of about ten years old who asked us to wait. Moments later the doctor appeared who said that he believed that I had an eye problem and invited Brian and me into the house where he also had his surgery. He examined my eye and after wiping it with a small swab, said that he had removed the offending speck but that my eye was so badly inflamed, I would not notice any difference until after I had a good night's sleep. We carried on to Glasgow and sure enough I had a miserable evening but the next morning all was well and everything was back to normal. Whilst there we visited Edinburgh and on arriving back were told that Brian's cousin, who was a teacher but working as a guide for a coach tour company during the school holidays, had acquired two spare tickets for the Edinburgh Tattoo so off we went back to Edinburgh on the coach for the tattoo.

We had decided to go home via Whitley Bay and had been offered a bed for the night by Mary, the widow of my cousin George. The journey there was wet, torturous, miserable and we did not arrive until after dark, having probably gone miles out of our way on the then new Newcastle Ring Road. We were relieved to get into a nice warm house and even happier to get into a nice warm bed. The following day we set off home after first visiting various relatives of mine and patching up a leak in the exhaust pipe on the scooter, with an old duster covered with a beer can all fastened on with a length of twisted wire. We did eventually arrive home safely, ready to resume our normal lives.

As the new academic year was starting, I enrolled for a German Grammar, Year One course at the Lancaster and Morecambe College of Further Education and my first lesson took place towards the end of September. The teacher was a German man probably in his mid-sixties caller Herr Edler. I realised shortly after I had started that I should have gone for a conversational course first as I had no vocabulary and was trying to reconcile the grammar with vocabulary at the same time from scratch but nevertheless I battled on. Firstly we learnt how to pronounce the letters of the alphabet and then learned to count. One advantage about learning grammar was that we learned how to read and write German and quickly learned all of the rules of pronunciation depending on the order of the letters within the words, as in German, unlike English, this is a constant rule and never changes. Eventually I started to really enjoy the course and managed to improve my vocabulary by buying German periodicals where I could find them and following a German course, which happened to be on television at that time.

During the summer not too much had been going on at with The Footlights Club but once into September I started going to the Grand Theatre much more again and enjoying the social life that went with it. The shop remained busy and everything was ticking along happily until the 19th November when I woke up that morning with excruciating stomach ache and feeling very sick. There was no way that I could go to work and I told my mother that I was sure that I would feel better as the day went along. This did not happen and gradually I felt more ill until I could bear it no longer and asked her to call the doctor. He arrived mid-afternoon and after examining me, diagnosed appendicitis and said that he would go straight home and ring for an emergency ambulance. About half an hour later the ambulance arrived and I was transported off to hospital with its blue light flashing on top. I was quickly admitted to the surgical ward where about three different doctors examined me, each one sticking their fingers up my bottom. A young nurse of about my age came with a bowl of water, a razor and shaved off my pubic hair. I was terribly embarrassed as I never envisaged that the first time a young lady of my age getting near to my private parts, was going to do that! I had always imagined it was going to be something considerably more romantic.

Several hours after the operation I woke up terribly thirsty but was not allowed a drink for two or three hours. Eventually two nurses came to get me out of bed but even when I moved slightly the pain was unbearable. Despite my protestations they said that it was for my own good even though I was in extreme pain. After about twenty four hours I felt a little more comfortable and was able to chat to some of my fellow patients, many who were much more ill than me and I felt a little guilty as I was on the mend and some of them probably never would be.

After three days, I was sent to a nursing home to convalesce for a spell and by then I was feeling a lot better. The staff were wonderful but I did not like the regime, I rebelled and am ashamed to say that I was a very difficult patient. I refused to go for an afternoon sleep when I was not tired and stayed up as late as possible watching television as I was still not tired. Eventually I was declared fit and sent home with instructions not to go back to work for six weeks and to see my doctor the following week. When I saw the doctor I complained that I was getting bored with nothing to do and begged him to sign me off, so I could return to work. He said that I was doing very well and that I could go back the following week as long as I promised not to lift or stretch for six weeks. I was off work for a total of seventeen days which in those days was considered something of a record after having an appendectomy.

By the time that I got back to work the Christmas rush had started and Mr Robertson made no secret of the fact that he was pleased to see me back and that my absence had caused him great inconvenience. The Footlights had got underway with the annual pantomime and I was soon back helping with this Christmas production, albeit without heavy lifting or stretching. After recovering from the operation I was feeling so much better and realised that I had probably been going down with the problem for quite some time beforehand. I felt so much better than I had done for two or three years and suddenly my appetite had increased to a level that I had never experienced before.

I had a quiet Christmas and New Year visiting a few friends

over the holidays but no riotous living this time, as I was still really convalescing and taking care of myself whilst my operation wound was healing.

1966

This year proved to be less eventful than the previous two years had been – there were no trips or educational visits imminent to camera manufacturers and my life at work was settling down to a steady routine. I had been working for four years in my job and was very confident in most aspects of it. Mr Robertson had occasionally left me in charge whilst he had a day or two off and gradually I was taking on more responsibility at work whilst Mr Robertson was easing off a little. I had no idea what the future held but hoped that as the Robertsons had no children, they would consider letting me run the shop when they decided to retire. At this point in time Mr Robertson was only sixty two years old and Mrs Robertson sixty five.

John Talbot and Pat were still working with me and John and I were still doing the odd things together socially. It was about now that he had joined the Bolton-le-Sands players and the production that they were about to start working on was called 'One Wild Oat' by Vernon Sylvaine. They were looking for a lead man and John asked if I would be interested in helping them out. I explained to John that as much as I enjoyed amateur dramatics, there was no way that I could act in the production, especially as the lead man, but eventually I was persuaded to take a lesser part and John took that of the lead man. It was an enjoyable experience and I made many friends there, a few of whom are still left today.

John also persuaded me to go to Cheshire with him to attend events held by a group who called themselves 'Moral Re-Armament' an organisation previously known as 'The Oxford Group'. It was basically a group of pacifists who believed that through total honesty, unselfishness and treating everyone alike they could change the world for the better with everyone trusting each other. John had by now had passed his driving test and acquired a Morris 1000 car so getting to Cheshire was no problem. The meetings were held in the grounds of a very large country house called 'Turley Garth' near Tarporley and the people that I met were all lovely people but despite going about three times, I realised that I was not going to change the world. I have, however, tried to live my life according to the values that they embrace although I know that I am not a good enough person not to have the occasional lapse, so probably did not deserve to be one of their members.

My dad had a friend who was selling an Ariel Arrow 250cc motorcycle which needed some work doing on it and I was interested. I had recently purchased for three pounds and ten shillings a Norton ES2 500cc motorcycle with sidecar from Philip Bowker's dad who owned a garage, had towed it in and had been given the log book in lieu of payment for the tow. This small price was to cover the towing fee only, as his dad said he would not make a profit out of me. My dad and I had got the Norton working ok but I was still quite slim, small and did not have the strength to handle this contraption on a long run so had sold it for twenty pounds. This, along with the proceeds from the sale of my Sun motorcycle, paid for the Ariel and after a spell in our cellar stripping and rebuilding the engine, the Ariel Arrow was up and running. This bike was a much better proposition for a long run and before long I travelled on it to Stoke-on-Trent to stay with my pal David Rack who had just purchased a Morris Mini car, having passed his driving test a month or two previously.

I was still doing my cinema photography and going to the pictures at least once a week as well as German evening classes and The Footlights club. I had recently become friends with a youth of similar age to me called David Silver who worked as a hairdresser at a shop on Ffrances Passage about four shops away from ours. Dave used to come with me to the cinema on my free pass and we had become really good friends. His dad was on the committee of The Borough Working Men's Club situated in Dalton Square, Lancaster and Dave was already a member. I was invited to join so after the cinema we could just pop across the road and have a drink before we went home.

Bill Shand's mother had returned and Bill went home, astonished to find that he had a little sister. Mrs Shand had told no one before she left that she was pregnant and had gone off to have the baby without family distractions but now that she had returned our lives got back to normal. It seemed funny at the time because Bill had become so much part of our family, we missed him after he went. His brother Robert had been staying with another family two streets away from us so Robert also went home at the same time as Bill.

Dave Silver was very keen on football so he and a workmate called Nigel Austin often used to go to Blackpool, Preston or Blackburn to watch the football. Like me, Dave and Nigel worked on Saturdays so we could usually only go to evening fixtures and whenever we did so, a stop off at a pub on the way back was obligatory. Occasionally we would also go to a cabaret in an establishment called The Queens at Cleveleys, then on into Blackpool, drinking at various pubs. On one occasion Nigel took a wrong turning and found himself driving down tram lanes against the flow of trams from which we could not escape for about half a mile but fortunately no tram came along. Another time he jumped a set of red traffic lights whilst speeding excessively out of Blackpool and we were chased by the police for about ten miles until we hid in a lay-by amongst some trees until the coast was clear. These were good times but we realised that our luck would not hold out indefinitely so gradually these nights out were curtailed.

During the early summer Dave Rack arrived in his Mini and came to stay with his granny. We had a few trips out, one being to Blackpool during the daytime but this time no alcohol was involved as Dave, like me, did not drink and drive. One evening he told me that he was going to Blackpool on his own. I don't know why he wanted to be alone and I never asked him why but off he went. About an hour later he returned in an AA rescue van but without his car. On the way to Blackpool he had crashed the car and written it off but he was completely unhurt so hung on for a few days before his dad could make the journey from Stoke-on-Trent to pick him up to take him home.

In June once again I went to Treasonfield Farm at Barbon to help the Martins with their haymaking and enjoyed the work just as much as I had done before. They now had two children and the new baby was called Alison, a sister for Christine who was growing up fast. This year was not as much of an effort as my skills learned from last year were still with me and I was able to pull my weight with the work involved. It was so good to be out in the beautiful countryside working with the constant aroma of fresh grass and hay in the evening light and every time I catch a smell of hay even now, my memories go straight back to those happy times spent helping Henry and Barbara Martin with their haymaking.

I suggested to Dave Silver that we might have a day or two in Whitley Bay and go on my bike. Dave was agreeable to this so we booked a bed and breakfast guest house at 6 Edwards Road, Whitley Bay and stayed there. I wanted to stay at that house as it was right next door to number four where my grandparents had brought up their family and my dad had lived. Latterly my Uncle Archie and Aunt Dora who lived there had recently moved out, after retiring to a small village called Horncliffe just outside Berwick-on-Tweed. Whilst staying there we had a trip up to Berwick to visit my cousin Kath who now lived in a hamlet called Velvet Hall very close to her parents at Horncliffe. Eric was now completely out of Kath's life after her marriage to David Allen. David was a delightful man with a gentle Scottish accent, typical as you will find in the border regions. This was the first time that I had met him and I took an instant liking to him as he was of an obviously gentle disposition but capable of dealing with the whims of Kath should she get out of hand! He was a wonderful father to Susan, thought the world of her and treated her as if she was his own daughter; he was a remarkable man and Kath was so lucky to have him.

We returned from our holiday on a hot late summer's day and popped into a pub in West Auckland for a drink as being togged up in motorcycling gear in the heat, we were thirsty, so I had a pint of lemonade and Dave a pint of beer. Shortly afterwards we were on the A66 road which had just been re-surfaced with loose gravel when the car in front of us had to brake suddenly causing me also to brake. Although the wheels of the bike locked, the bike didn't stop skidding along the gravel, resulting in me crashing into the rear of the car in front. The accident was not my fault but was my responsibility as are most accidents when someone is hit from behind. The result was a ten pound fine and three penalty points on my licence for driving without due care and attention issued by the Magistrates Court in Barnard Castle. I was so glad that I had only had a soft drink prior to the accident as the penalty could have been so much worse.

My brother Fred was now starting school and went to the same school as me, Dallas Road School. Several of my old teachers were still there but Fred was a lot more fortunate than me in getting a young blonde teacher called Jean Robinson who showed a good deal more patience with Fred than my old teacher, Miss Dobson, had shown to me. Fred's teacher and her family were customers at the shop so I suddenly started to recognise them when they came in and soon got to know her and her family quite well.

My parents were increasingly getting worried about me riding a motor bike, especially after what had recently happened so my dad said that he would look out for a car and teach me to drive. Just after my twentieth birthday he found an old Ford Popular with a three speed gearbox and a dinge in the roof. The car was, however, a good runner and shortly after we got it he sprayed it a bright shade of red for me. There were not many bright coloured cars then, especially old ones, so this suited me as it looked quite smart. I had never driven a car before, only tractors, but this was very different to a tractor. Getting used to road conditions was not a problem as I had motorcycled all over the country but I did have a problem with being closed into a car after feeling the wind on my face when motorcycling and it took me a while to get used to that. I had a week's holiday due to me which I took in November so my dad and I went to stay with Mary in Whitley Bay. I did all of the driving as the object of the holiday was to get as much practice in as possible prior to my test and anyway I knew the roads better than my dad as they had changed so much since his days of living in the north east of England. We drove to Horncliffe to see my Uncle Archie; his wife, my Auntie Dora, had now died so he was living on his own with Kath keeping an eye on him from only a couple of miles away. My dad and he chatted for about half an hour before it was time to return to Whitley Bay. It turned out that Uncle Archie also had a similar model of Ford Popular car so he gave us some spares that he did not need for which we were grateful. He said that he would show us a short cut back to the main A1 road south, so he led the way and we all stopped outside The Cat Pub just south of Berwick to shake hands and say farewell. As we drove off my Uncle Archie stood outside

The Cat and waved until we were out of sight. He died just three months later and my enduring memory of him is waving at us there and every time that I drive past The Cat, even to this day, that vision of my Uncle Archie stood waving is still with me. Soon afterwards I took my driving test and failed on one item of driving but as two things had to be wrong, the examiner spent over ten minutes with me asking an enormous amount of questions on the highway code until he caught me out by asking where on a steep hill is the warning sign, top or bottom. I was not sure so he now had the two faults needed to fail me. I put in for my second test immediately and during that test, I had a genuine emergency stop when a child ran out straight in front of the car to which I immediately responded by screeching to a halt. Afterwards, I was asked only two questions on the Highway Code then was told that I had passed and was congratulated on my genuine emergency stop to avoid hitting the child.

My life was still busy with all of my social activities including my German class for which I was now into my second year. It was coming along slowly as I was still not getting enough vocabulary to go with the grammar. I had tried to come into contact with Germans as much as possible but in 1966, there were not that many opportunities in England to do that. I was still busy with all of my other activities and not spending much of my spare time at home. My brother Fred was now five years old and I was starting to enjoy his company as well as his toys, which were becoming more interesting as he was becoming older. The shop as ever remained busy and John Talbot decided that he was leaving for work in the south of England, back to where he had come from originally, so shortly we would be looking for a new assistant.

A little time before Christmas, I had met a new girlfriend and much of the Christmas festivities were spent at her house along with her rather strict and suspicious parents. I do not intend to go into much detail here as she is, to the best of my knowledge, still alive and was sexually experienced before she met me, hence her suspicious parents. As much as it might be every chap's dream to have a girlfriend constantly wanting sex, it was not for me as at that time she was very vulnerable and whilst I enjoyed a kiss, a cuddle and the odd grope, I did not want the full experience. I was not in love with her and to give her what she wanted would have been to take advantage of her vulnerability and to take away the mystery and enjoyment which I only wanted to share with the girl with whom, eventually, I might fall in love. Not long afterwards, I told her that I wanted to go my own way and break off the relationship as I knew that it could go no further. She was very upset and at first would not accept it but when she realised that I meant it, she relented, although for a while afterwards would not speak to me if we passed in the street. Eventually she found someone else, left home and was ok with me again.

1967

A t the shop we were now looking for a new assistant to replace John Talbot who was leaving to become a photographer near London and he came in the shape of Bill Cowell. At first Bill was very quiet almost to the point of being shy but behind that deceptive facade was a very enthusiastic photographer with a great gift for pulling things to pieces and restoring them to excellent condition. Many of his interests besides photography were similar to mine, amateur radio being one of them; he was also good with clocks and many other small mechanical things. He lived with his mother and sister in a big house in Morecambe, along with his grandparents who owned the house. He went out very little in his spare time and therefore occupied it by taking things to pieces to discover how they worked, hence his talent for mending and restoring all sorts of gadgets. His sister was quite pretty and I did take her out for a short while but one day she said to me that she did not feel that our relationship was going anywhere and I agreed with her, so we both went our separate ways.

The time was approaching for me to take my final examinations which were held in London. My practical work had already been submitted by post but at the end of March I had to go and sit a two and a half hour written examination and a one hour oral later in the same day. The results for this arrived back about two weeks later and to my horror, I had failed the written examination; too much going out and other distractions had taken their toll, so I would have to go back the following year to do it again. I had passed both my practical and oral examination so that was going to count for the next time only but this concentrated my mind into paying more attention to my work and a little less on leisure activities.

Mr Robertson decided to take a holiday and left me in charge of everything. I was already familiar with cashing up and banking the takings as he had already taken a day or two off here and there previously, obviously to get me used to dealing with that side of the business. There were no problems and we had been very busy so he was pleased and suggested that I should take a bookkeeping course at the college when the new academic year started in September, to which I agreed. He also decided that every Monday night, I should go to his house for tea and then help him with the books for an hour or two, so that I would become familiar with the complete running of the business. This I enjoyed immensely as Mrs Robertson gave me things that I liked for tea and introduced me to coleslaw which I had never had before but have always enjoyed since. Now that I was going to the house every week, I got to know Mrs Robertson better than ever before and found her a lot more humorous that she had originally appeared and soon she was spoiling me rotten, I suspect in lieu of the children that she never had.

Brian and Pat had become engaged some time ago; now they were getting married and Brian had asked me to be his best man. This is something that I had never done before and I was pretty nervous about everything concerned with the wedding, especially my speech. When eventually the day came, the wedding was excellent and went off without a hitch. The reception was held in the function room above the Alexandra Hotel, Lancaster and the time came for my speech. Afterwards I felt that I had not done a terribly good job or Brian justice as my jokes all fell on stony ground as I was not really on the same wavelength as the guests and I am sure that the inexperience of youth had prevailed. I don't remember them having a honeymoon as they had just purchased a brand new house at Broadacre, Caton so probably needed all of their money to start up home together.

I was now twenty years old and on my next birthday would be twenty one, which meant that many of my friends of a similar age to me were having twenty first birthday parties. I was invited to go to Stockport to celebrate Dave Rack's twenty first birthday in May. The family had decided that they would all stay with his Auntie Marion and Uncle Bob as they had a very big house with enough room to sleep all of us after the celebrations. His granny had already gone there a week or two earlier as she was now spending more time away from home with one or other of her children as she was in her eighties and was dearly loved by them, owing to her easy going disposition and youthful mind. I caught the bus to Manchester and then the local service to Stockport where I made my way to the house and met up with all of the family. I was the only friend of David's there but celebrated with the rest of the family by being treated to a wonderful meal at a lovely restaurant about ten miles away and for the first time in my life had a proper steak.

Not long afterwards Dave's granny arrived home and a few weeks later Dave came to stay, driving up from Stoke in his Triumph Spitfire sports car, which had an open top and looked absolutely superb. The shop had now started closing all day on Wednesdays so on a Tuesday night after I had finished work, Dave suggested that we return to Stoke-on-Trent just overnight and he would drive me back to Lancaster the following day. I was definitely up for this idea but Dave said that he would have to ring his dad first, as he had promised to do so if setting off back home. We stopped at the telephone box on Lancaster bus station for Dave to ring home, as neither my parents nor his granny had a phone; we then made our way to the M6 motorway for the journey. Once on the motorway Dave passed everything on the road and for much of the time we were cruising at ninety miles per hour. In about an hour we were in Stoke and Dave decided that it was not wise to go straight home as his dad would realise that we had been speeding if he arrived too early. We spent about half an hour looking in shop windows before going back to Dave's house where we were greeted by his dad who accused him of speeding. 'I expected you back before this,' he said, 'and the only way it has taken you this long is to put on some time before you got here, so I know that you were speeding; don't do it again.' We had been found out; with the inexperience of youth and lack of parenthood, we did not realise just how smart that the older generation could be!

I was keeping busy with my cinema photography and had been asked to go along one evening as they were getting a visit from a British film star called June Thorburn. It was a very busy event and besides me, all of the local newspaper photographers were there. We were all took it in turns to photograph June Thorburn who politely posed for each of us. She looked beautiful and very glamorous in a tight white sparkly dress and was pleasantly quiet and patient until we had all finished. It was such a terrible shock later in the year, to learn that she had been killed in an aeroplane crash in Sussex on a return trip from Spain.

During the late summer I decided that I would like to have a trip to the North East and invited my friend Dave Silver to come along. I prearranged for us to stay one night with Mary before we moved on to Seahouses where I knew we could spend a second night in the car, if we tucked it well into the sand dunes out of sight of the road. We had a very comfortable night with Mary and a less comfortable one sleeping in the car the following night. Early next morning we were awoken by two attractive young ladies who were looking for a lift to Belford, had somehow spotted us and wondered if we were going in that direction. We immediately said that we were, put them in the back of the car and took them to Belford. It turned out that they were hotel receptionists who had been at a social event in Seahouses the night before and had missed the last bus back to Belford. After we dropped them off, we returned to Seahouses before setting off back home later on in the day. On the way back we got stuck in a horrendous traffic jam outside of Barnard Castle. It was a really hot day and some cars had pulled into what looked like a field with a lot of hard standing. It turned out that it was where the army sometimes had a camp site but at the time that we were there, it was not being used. We and many other motorists pulled off the road, put our cars on the hard standing and we both fell asleep on the grass while sunbathing. An hour or so later we awoke to find that the traffic jam had gone, so we got back in the car and carried on until we arrived home.

September was soon upon us and it was again time to consider what I wanted to do about my German studies. I decided this year to do a conversational course which was being held at Ryelands House in Ryelands Park, Lancaster. It turned out that the two years of German grammar under my belt had been very useful because it had enabled me to read and write the language. Others who had been doing conversational longer than me had more vocabulary but were now being held back because they had not been taught the basic foundations of German grammar. With the new vocabulary that I was learning, my German was now improving quickly but I knew even then that the only way to really improve it was to go to Germany again. I also had enrolled at the college for a GCE 'Principles of Accounts' course which was the bookkeeping studies that Mr Robertson had asked me to do. This along with Monday nights doing bookkeeping at

Mr Robertson's house was tying me up for three evenings a week but somehow, I still found time to go to the cinema, get along to the Grand Theatre occasionally and have a Saturday night out in the pub with my mates. In those days the pubs closed at ten thirty with ten minutes drinking up time but we could often stay a bit later in the Borough Club if we chose to be there.

My friend Eric Rogerson had met a girl, got engaged and was getting married. Eric was temporarily a bus conductor on the Ribble buses and his older brother Jimmy was a bus driver for the same company. He also had a younger brother called Alan but what his occupation was, I cannot remember. Two nights before the wedding, I was invited out to Eric's stag night and had to be at Lancaster Bus Station for 7.00pm. When I got there I found that there was a party of about twenty of us and a single decker Ribble bus with a driver who had been hired for the occasion, the driver knowing the Rogerson brothers, being a work colleague. We were driven to 'The Queens Bar' at Cleveleys, near Blackpool, the same spot where Dave Silver, his friend Nigel and myself had misspent some of our evenings in the past. We stayed in the cabaret bar for about an hour and after having two or three drinks then went around to another part of the building where there was a disco in full swing. To our surprise it was full of lovely girls and hardly any men. It turned out that several of the girls worked together at a local supermarket and were having a girls' night out and until we arrived there had been a shortage of men. We spent the rest of the night in the disco, drinking and dancing and by the end of the evening most of the men were pretty drunk, including the bus driver! Every one of us had found a girlfriend for the evening including Eric who was getting married two days later and when it was time to leave, invited all of the girls to get onto the coach for a lift home. We gave every one of the girls a lift and had to prise Eric away from his girlfriend as they were passionately snogging on the back seat of the bus. By the time that we had dropped off all of the girls it was getting into the early hours of the morning, so the driver took the Preston road to pick up the M6 motorway at Broughton near Preston, as in those days there was no motorway link directly into Blackpool.

We were no sooner on the motorway when the driver started to perform all sorts of stunt driving, one foot on the steering wheel and the other on the accelerator waving at the cars that were passing us. Jimmy Rogerson being a bus driver became alarmed at this and eventually persuaded the driver to pull into the hard shoulder and stop the bus. When the bus stopped Jimmy assisted the driver to sit further back in the bus with a view to taking over, as, although drunk, he was not as drunk as the driver. Whilst the bus was stopped the engine was still running with the driver's seat momentarily empty, Eric slid into the seat and started to drive the bus away. The problem was that Eric was not a bus driver, he didn't even have a car licence therefore had difficulty driving the bus in a straight line. At this Jimmy became even more alarmed than before and now everyone else on the bus was getting worried. Despite unanimously worried voices from the whole of the passengers Eric was not deterred and we went a few miles before he could be persuaded to stop the bus and let Jimmy take over. When we reached Forton Services just outside Lancaster, the coach pulled in, as everyone needed the toilets and most of us were hungry. Eric's younger brother Alan was feeling pretty ill by now and when he reached the toilets was extremely sick and on turning round to leave, found himself face to face with a clergyman! Despite the late hour, food was still being served so most of us had egg and chips which did help a little to sober us up. I don't really remember what happened after that so assume that I was dropped off in Lancaster to make the rest of my way home.

Two days later the wedding took place at St. Wilfred's Church at Halton, just outside Lancaster, and the reception was held in the newly opened Halton Social Club, where the bride's father was a founder member and on the committee. I had taken a day's holiday off work so enjoyed the day tremendously and no mention was made of our riotous time the night before last, in case various girlfriends, wives and especially the bride found out. We had the use of the club until midnight when everyone went home, most of us the worse for wear and for about twenty of us, it was for the second time within forty eight hours.

Not long afterwards my twenty first birthday was looming and my parents said that I could have a party, the first one for many years since the disaster of the air gun dart and the broken sofa. My mum made a pile of sandwiches and cakes and when completed we had a pretty respectable buffet. We had sourced a five gallon barrel of beer along with bottled gas and glasses so had beer on draught. There were also a few bottles of other alcohol around but I don't remember any wine as most of my friends didn't drink it then. One or two neighbours were invited including Mrs Teale, Dave Rack's granny, and Dave drove all of the way from Stoke-on-Trent just for an hour or two to wish me a happy birthday. He had to drive back straight away as he was working the next morning, so did not partake in any of the alcohol on offer. By today's standards it would seem to be a pretty tame affair but then it was great, it was a party and was very similar to the sort of twenty first birthday parties that my friends had. My parents bought me a superb transistor radio with FM, good in those days and I received lots of other wonderful gifts including a pewter tankard and a good road atlas which I used for a few years afterwards to get me around the country.

Christmas was a pretty hectic affair with my Grand Theatre activities and all of the social life that went with it, plus events at The Borough Club and various gatherings at friends' houses. New Year's Eve was spent at Brian's parents' house as I was firmly on the invitation list of his Scottish mum and enjoyed the Hogmanay party that she always held.

1968

A t the beginning of the year I had also been contacted by a man
called Mr Wilkes representing The Lancashire Education
Committee asking if I would teach a twelve week course for adults
on 'Photography for Beginners'. This was to take place at Quernmore
School from 7.00pm to 9.00pm on a Tuesday night. I had never done
anything like this before but devised a syllabus based on 'The all in
one camera book' by W.D. Emanuel, a fellow traveller whom I was to
meet later in the year on my trip to Russia. I enjoyed doing this and
made an enormous amount of friends in the process. As I was not a
qualified teacher the pay was poor and I probably spent most of it on
materials to do practical demonstrations.

I had also started the year by making sure that this time I was
properly prepared for my final examinations as I did not want a
recurrence of last year's failure. Once again I had to go to London to
sit the written examination but not having to do the oral again finished
much earlier than I had done the year before. I had looked up my
friend Ken Ward who lived in Woodford Bridge working at 'St John's
Open Air School', a private school for boys, and arranged to stay the
night before travelling into London the next day for my examination.

This time I travelled by train which was much faster than by coach so I arrived home later on the same day that I had sat my exam. My hard work had paid off as this time I passed and from that moment was no longer an apprentice but a fully trained 'Retail Photographic Salesman' accredited by The Photographic Dealers Association and trained by G. L. Robertson. My pay suddenly increased but I cannot now remember now how much I earned except I do remember feeling a lot better off. It must have also been beneficial for my parents who took money off me for my board and lodgings and it was always a third of what I earned.

From the end of last year and through the spring this year, I had entered a sales competition through the shop for a place on a trip to Russia. It was based on camera sales and the merits of a window display of Russian cameras and binoculars. I had pinched a pair of long black boots from my sister's wardrobe and put cotton wool around the top of them and placed them in the shop window surrounded by various Russian optics before photographing them for submission with my sales figures for the competition. My sister went looking for her boots one day and was furious when she found out that they were sitting in the shop window and demanded their return immediately. When she asked me why I had not sought permission first to borrow them, I told her that I knew that she would refuse and I needed them for the photograph but now that had been done she could have them back immediately.

Nothing happened for a while until one Friday afternoon we received a phone call at the shop from the representative of the Russian camera importers. It appeared that I had not won a place in the competition but had been thirty first out of thirty winners and was first on the reserve list. One of the winners had given back word at the eleventh hour and if I wanted a place, I could go on the trip as long as I could be in London for nine o'clock on Monday morning outside their offices, armed with my passport and two spare passport photographs. Another phone call to my friend Ken Ward secured me a bed and on Saturday afternoon I caught the train to London and then the underground to Woodford Green where he met me as we had about a mile or so to walk to Woodford Bridge. He explained to me that he was no longer allowed to have guests to stay after a fellow worker had sneaked his girlfriend in to stay the night and that they had been caught in bed together. We spent the remainder of the evening in the local pub called 'The Crown and Crocked Billett' then made our way back to 'St John's School' and after ensuring that the coast was clear, Ken sneaked me into his quarters, me sleeping on his settee. The following day when the coast was clear, Ken and I caught a bus to Walthamstow where I caught the underground into London to stay there on the Sunday night.

Monday morning I was outside the offices of the importers on Praed Street and when they opened, presented myself to the receptionist. A young employee explained to me that a visa would have to be obtained which was normally a lengthy process but his Russian boss, a man called Mr Ashmarin, had contacted his colleagues in the Russian Consulate who said that if we were there at nine thirty, a visa would be ready about three hours later. We duly arrived at the Russian Consulate as arranged and after a few checks were invited inside. The staff were solemn and the atmosphere grim and at first the man interviewing us said that it would be impossible to obtain a visa in under six weeks. The young man with me mentioned Mr Ashmarin and the name of another Russian who worked at the consulate and the man interviewing us disappeared. He eventually re-appeared, requesting my passport and the two spare photographs and said to return at twelve thirty when the visa should be ready and my passport would be returned. I was told by the young man who had arranged all of this to be back at his office at midday when we would return by taxi to the Russian Consulate and this is what happened. When we got there the mood was a little less sombre and my passport was returned along with a Russian entry and exit visa enabling me to go on the trip. I quickly had to grab some lunch as everyone was meeting at an assembly point at one thirty and we were bussed to Tilbury for embarkation on 'The Alexander Pushkin', a Russian ship which was to take us to Leningrad, now known by its original name of St. Petersburg.

When I got on board a member of the crew gave me a ticket that showed my cabin number which I made my way to, in order to shed my hand luggage. When I opened the door, there were two men sitting down with a bottle of whisky and full glasses. When they saw me they immediately filled another glass and invited me to join them. I explained that I was a little perplexed as this was supposed to be my cabin and the cabins only slept two. They explained that there had been a big mix up and that we all had to meet up about an hour later in one of the lounges, so in the meantime why not just sit down and enjoy the whisky and a chat. When they introduced themselves, one was a photographic dealer from St. Helens called Ken Farnham and the other Derek Hargreaves from Liverpool. Both had businesses considerably bigger than ours but nevertheless they were most friendly, out for a good time and were quite happy for me to tag along with them. After the meeting in the lounge area I was allocated another cabin which I was to share with a chap called Alf McDonough, a man considerably older than myself but very affable and with whom I got along fine. At six o'clock we all went off to the dining room where the food was incredible and of the likes of which I had never seen before, served by Russian staff who were polite but very restrained. It was probably about seven thirty before we had finished our meal and then I decided to explore the ship. By today's standards it would be considered very small for a cruise type ship but then it seemed large with several cafes and five bar areas. Not all were open at the same time but there was never a time when all were closed so one could get something to eat or drink at any time of the day or night. There was also a swimming pool and several decks with chairs and sun loungers so the whole experience just seemed to be getting better all of the time. Before going to bed, I met up with some of our party in one of the bars and had a drink or two before retiring.

When I woke the next morning and went for breakfast, everyone was talking about a storm in the night but it appears most people had been awoken by the tossing around of the ship. In my youth I was an extremely heavy sleeper and had not been disturbed so I had woken up very fresh, ready to face a new and exciting day. After lunch the ship put into Bremerhaven which I had no idea was going to happen but I was delighted, as now I had my very first opportunity to try out all of the German that I had been learning for almost three years. Although we only had about three hours ashore, I had the chance to walk around the town and to make some small purchases in the shops and, to my delight, my German was working and I could talk to people. I had to listen carefully as I could not understand everything that was coming back but I understood enough to get the gist of it and was thrilled that all my hard work was paying off and I was at last semi-bilingual. We were no sooner back on the ship and it was time for dinner, another wonderful experience awaited us and once again I sat in one of the bars later with several of our party quietly drinking, chatting and passing the time before going to bed.

The next day was hot and sunny so I got up early and went for a swim before breakfast but the water was really cold so I didn't stay in the pool for long. After breakfast I found a lounger and lay in the sun whilst we sailed down the Danish coast. From time to time Russian waiters brought drinks of beer and this was just heaven, drinking beer, lounging in the warm sunshine and I was sorry when I had to break off for lunch. During the afternoon I was buying a beer from one of the bars when an elderly German man spoke to me in German, thinking that I was a German. I explained to him that I was English but was learning German so welcomed the conversation and practice. We chatted for about half an hour and he asked me if I would like to return again in the evening to continue with our conversation so I said that I would. After another splendid dinner I made my way back to the bar and shortly afterwards he turned up so I bought him and myself a beer each. He immediately responded by buying each of us a whisky chaser and next time round he bought me a beer, so I was obliged to buy us both a whisky. The conversation eventually got around to the Second World War and here I was a little out of my depth as I had never knowingly spoken to a German who had fought the British. He did, however, make it very easy for me saying how horrible war was and how it should never have happened as most ordinary German people did not want it and he was sure that the British population in general felt just the same. I re-assured him that I thought that was exactly how it was and that most people everywhere just wanted to be friends and get on with their lives. That night I had a continuous German conversation lasting for about two and a half hours and for the last hour in particular I could feel the effects of the alcohol gradually but steadily taking its toll as we continued to consume the beer and whisky. Eventually I knew that I could not last out a lot longer so excused myself by saying it was past my bedtime and with great difficulty found my cabin, closed the door and collapsed unconscious on my bed.

When I woke up the next morning I was tucked up in bed in just my underclothes. Alf had come in and found me, sorted me out, as he realised that I was extremely drunk and had felt sorry for me. I felt absolutely dreadful and the very thought of breakfast made me feel even more ill. It took me all morning to get to a point where I could even contemplate lunch which I ate sparingly as I was still very fragile and did not get back to normal until I had eaten dinner that night. I kept well away from my German friend as I knew that it might well end up with a repeat performance which I knew that I could not handle as well as he, I being a relative beginner at drinking, against his extensive and lifetime experience.

The next day we were now well into the Baltic Sea which I found fascinating. This was the place where during the Second World War so many battles had been fought, great hardships endured and where so many men had died. We were sailing along on a calm sea in relative warmth on a comfortable ship with drinks in our hands, relaxing and enjoying the peace and luxury. How fortunate we were compared to those who had gone before as they probably never imagined what was to follow at their time of torture and we were so lucky to enjoy the fruits of their sacrifice. The evening was particularly beautiful and I sat outside for a long time before it got dark, if it ever properly did, as there always appeared to be a slight glow in the sky.

After I had got up the next day I felt cold and had to put on some warm clothes as the weather was suddenly very chilly. Late in the morning I went out on deck and it started sleeting. This came as a big shock as previously the weather had gone from hot to warm but no one had expected sleet. We were about to dock in Helsinki and after lunch had about three and a half hours ashore to explore the town. I teamed up with Ken Farnham and Derek Hargreaves again, so we all explored Helsinki together. Practically everyone spoke English, especially in the shops, and the Finnish girls were absolutely beautiful. Many of the shops were displaying posters sporting the British Union Flag as at that time there had been a promotion to buy British goods. Shortly before we made our way back to the ship, we spotted some children playing a game that we did not recognise in a playground and using a wooden ball. Whether by accident or on purpose I will never know but the ball was thrown hard in our direction, hitting Derek Hargreaves in the face and breaking his spectacles. Like me he was short sighted and his glasses were damaged beyond repair, so for the rest of the trip he had limited vision as a reminder of his trip to Helsinki.

Our last day on the ship was sailing up the Gulf of Finland towards Leningrad. Dinner was more spectacular than ever with several treats we had not seen before, particularly caviar which at home one could never afford to buy but was much more commonplace to the Russians, well at least the privileged ones. We retired early that night as breakfast the next day was going to be early, with us having to disembark at what normally would have been breakfast time.

The atmosphere at breakfast was strange – an elderly lady came to sit on our table who was Russian born but had left Russia with her parents and had fled to America during the Russian revolution. She seemed completely American but was suddenly attacked by nerves when she realised that she was going to set foot on her native soil for the first time since being a child and seemed very apprehensive about what she might have to face with the Russian officials at immigration. Our waitress on the ship was trying unsuccessfully to hold back her tears as she plainly was not looking forward to arriving home. We tried to comfort her but all she would say was that we would not understand!

Going through immigration was a nightmare as the Russian officials opened lots of cases, looking for all sorts of forbidden items. Back in the days of communism, items that to us seem so innocent, such as The Holy Bible, were considered subversive and anyone caught trying to bring one into the country could get a prison sentence. As it happened, my case was never opened but I don't think that anything that I had would have upset the authorities anyway. Eventually we were rounded up and put onto a coach, which took us to our hotel. On the way, I was astonished to see a team of short but sturdy muscular ladies digging up the road. I did know that in Russia women were used as labourers but I had forgotten and to suddenly witness it came as a great shock. It brought me up with a jolt as to the differences in our cultures and how very lucky we were in Great Britain. On the coach we were given all sorts of instructions and advice, in particular under no circumstances to exchange western currency for Roubles on the streets as this was black marketing which could carry a prison sentence if caught. Selling clothes or anything else for Roubles was almost as bad, as foreigners were only allowed to obtain Roubles through official outlets and to keep any paperwork safe, to prove that the transactions were approved by the State. We were also told not to photograph railway stations, airports or individual people, particularly policemen, but if the photograph was a general scene containing lots of people even including policemen in the distance, that was then permissible.

On arrival at our hotel we were quickly allocated rooms and I had one all to myself. It was a little austere but the bedding was clean and it was certainly adequate with the exception of no plug for the bath or the wash basin. We were given about two hours to settle in before lunch but I was ready long before that so decided to explore. On the way out I met one of my fellow travellers so we went out on the street together. I had hardly got outside when I was politely accosted by an English speaking Russian who asked if I would give him a one pound note for five Roubles. I said absolutely no so then he offered me ten Roubles, four times the official exchange rate. I explained that this was forbidden and that he must know that but he said that he had got away with it many times before if it was done carefully by each of us palming our respective notes, shaking hands and each of us slipping our notes into the others hand, then no one would realise. This we did and suddenly I had ten Roubles and he had disappeared. My friend was astonished at the ease of this transaction and when we met our fellow travellers at lunchtime about half of us had done a black market transaction but at that point, I had secured the best deal! At first this seemed like a great way to make our money go a long way but we soon realised that when we were to leave Russia, the authorities would demand to see the paperwork showing how many Roubles that we had purchased. If it came to considerably less in value than the purchased goods in our suitcases, there would be proof of black marketeering, so at that point my black market activities stopped.

After lunch we were taken out on a coach trip around Leningrad. Some parts were very interesting but others were boring. They seemed to take great delight in showing us the amount of redundant churches which had gone out of use owing to lack of finance. Apparently each church had to be self-supporting so wealthier ones could not support poorer ones, which meant the Russian state by stealth was gradually trying to eliminate Christianity. We were also taken to outside of the Winter Palace where we were allowed to stroll for about twenty minutes. I felt that I was taking a step back in time as I had seen so many historical movies of this spot where the soldiers during the revolution had gunned down the public who were trying to storm the palace. I felt the atmosphere, which for me still existed, and knew that I was privileged to be here at that time as relatively few westerners had visited since the revolution had taken place in 1917.

We were taken back to the hotel for dinner which was not very good, most of the food being undercooked, semi cooked and sometimes raw. Sadly this was to be the theme of most hotel food that we ate in Russia as they seemed to have no idea of western tastes but what they were serving was not authentic Russian food and so much of what we were offered was almost inedible. That night many of us went to bed hungry hoping that breakfast the next morning had more to offer.

Breakfast was probably the best meal of the day as bacon and eggs were available but I was warned not to touch what I thought was a glass of milk as it turned out to be sour cream. After breakfast we were taken first to a camera shop in a shopping area where we were allowed to handle many models of equipment that we had never seen before, as they had not been imported into the UK. All of the equipment that we saw was Russian as the regime of the day would not allow any non-Russian items to be sold in the shops, except tourist shops. Tourist shops would not accept Roubles but only other western currency, hence the demand for black market pounds and dollars, which would then allow the Russians to purchase goods otherwise not available to them. After our visit to the camera shop we were then taken to a camera and optical factory. As the coach pulled up to the factory gate, a female sentry with a rifle over her shoulder stopped our coach and spoke to our driver before allowing us to continue. We were then ushered into a building and up a flight of stairs and into a dingy room resembling an old fashioned classroom. There were two lines of tables starting at the front of the room and ending at the back with about a dozen tables in each line. At each table sat a person with a box of camera parts in front of them and production started at the top table with the bare camera body being passed back to the table behind, with each person adding more parts until it reached next to the last table when the camera construction was complete. On the last table the camera was put into a case and along with an instruction book placed into a box which was then sealed with a gummed label; this was first wetted on a porcelain roller before being stuck on the box. These two lines competed with each other and each time a completed box came off the end of the production line the last worker put up their hand and a score of the total that day was constantly updated on a blackboard at the front of the line. This was a rudimentary process to say the least but the Cosmic 35mm Cameras that were being produced were basic, very reliable and performed extremely well. I had sold many of them in our shop with a high degree of customer satisfaction. We were then led back down the stairs and shown a large open fronted building behind the one that we had just been inside, where at that time the world's second largest optical telescope was being built and was in fact almost completed. We were given lunch and then taken back to the hotel and given free time for the rest of the day.

On leaving the hotel and walking down to the end of the road, I was on the Nevski Prospect and owing to its extreme length decided to catch a tram – a big mistake as it turned out! I waited at the stop and the tram took on several passengers but as it was very full with standing room only, I made my way up to the middle of the coach where there was a large gap next to a ticket machine. There was no conductor and I must have looked puzzled as another passenger made hand signals to indicate that I must get my own ticket from the machine and deposit four Kopecks into the honesty box. This I did but moments after there was a tap on my shoulder and four Kopecks were handed to me and again I looked puzzled. More hand signals indicated for me to put the money in the box take a ticket and hand it back down the tram, I suddenly realised why no one wanted to stand next to the ticket machine as by doing so I had become the unofficial tram conductor taking money and handing out tickets, which I had to do several times more. I decided to get off the tram at the next stop to avoid this, so pushed my way to the door, got off the tram and walked the rest of the way to the end of Nevski Prospect until I reached Admiralty Arch on the opposite side of the square to The Winter Palace.

I spent some time again soaking up the atmosphere before making my way back, but this time walked the whole way, going into some of the shops and purchasing a few gifts to take home. Most shops were dingy and had a limited selection of goods available and in those you had to look at the price ticket of each item that you wanted to buy, add up the cost and go to a kiosk to pay for them, where you were handed a receipt. Armed with the receipt you went to the counter, indicated to the assistant what goods you required, handed back the receipt and then you were given the goods that you wanted. Only in one shop that I found, a music and record shop, could you decide what you wanted and pay the assistant as you would do at home. Shopping in Russia was a complicated task and must have been frustrating for local people, taking up a lot more time than was necessary, but this was a way of ensuring that the staff could not have a hand in the till, as only one person was responsible for the money. When I ended up back at the hotel several of my fellow travellers were at the bar so I joined them for a few drinks.

That evening we were taken to the ballet but not having eaten too much of the unappetising meal and having had a few afternoon drinks, I could hardly keep awake. This was a shame as the ballet was quite beautiful and although I had never fancied going to the ballet previously, what I do remember was the sense of occasion that impressed me but my state of mind that evening did not do justice to how superb the event must have been. In the interval we were given Russian ice cream which is apparently famous for its quality; this was stunning and probably the best that I have ever had. At the end of the evening we were returned to our hotel by coach and it turned out that most of us had nodded off during the performance. I deeply regret having done this, spoiling what should have been the most memorable experience of a lifetime. By the time that I went to bed I had woken up a little and had found a recent English newspaper, 'The Daily Worker', which I read from cover to cover being so desperate for something to read as I must have been desperate to read that.

After breakfast the next day, we were taken for a three hour trip to The Hermitage to see an amazing amount of works of art from every famous artist and sculptor imaginable. It was impossible to see everything as the collection is so vast but the amount of treasures there is beyond imagination and the beauty of the building is breathtaking. How the Tsar and his family must have lived is beyond comprehension. We were given lunch but I cannot remember where, then whisked off to the Catherine Palace for part of the afternoon. During the Second World War it had been taken over by the invading German troops and towards the end of the war when they retreated, it was ransacked, vandalised and torched. When we were there it had been half restored but we allowed to see the unrestored part, which was a blackened shell. We then went round the restored part which was amazing and had been renovated by craftsmen helped by art students who gave their spare time freely as their duty to the State. The restoration was completely authentic as it was being put back to its original state with the help of pre-war photographs which had been taken before the palace had been almost destroyed. It was then back to the hotel for an early tea as we were catching an evening flight to take us on the next leg of our tour, visiting Moscow.

On the airport complex, one of our party uncovered his camera and took a photograph which initiated a lot of shouting from a man wearing a red armband who wrenched the camera from his hand, opened it and ripped out the roll of film. The camera was handed back with even more shouting and although no one understood what he was saying, there was little doubt as to what he meant.

Our aeroplane was operated by Aeroflot Russian Airlines and whilst in flight the English speaking pilot proudly announced over the public address system that the plane was a Russian-built TU144 jet model which could be adapted for use as a passenger aircraft or as a bomber! When over Moscow we descended at a rate that I have never experienced before or since and everyone clutched their ears because of the pain experienced owing to the fast descent. By the time we got to the hotel it was dark. We were given a light supper and then shown to our rooms, again austere and again with no plugs, but one of our number had found a solution to the lack of bath plugs. All of us had taken Kodak film for our cameras and the plastic top of the container holding the film fitted the Russian bath plugholes perfectly so we were all now able to have a bath.

The next morning we were scheduled to visit a Russian camera factory but when breakfast was over we were told that the trip had been cancelled and no reason was given. We were asked to go to a large room to have a group photograph taken by a professional photographer whose camera caused a lot of interest as it was of Russian manufacture and a model that we had never seen before. We were then taken around Moscow by coach to see many of its most famous landmarks before being given the rest of the day free to wander around as we pleased. I spent a couple of hours meandering around Red Square and areas adjacent including The Gum Department Store on the opposite side of Red Square to The Kremlin. We had to be back at the hotel by mid-afternoon as we were being taken to a special dinner party as guests of the Russian camera manufacturers and be properly dressed for the occasion in our lounge suits. The spread was magnificent with several courses and lashings of different caviars on the tables provided as a snack. For every two people there was a large bottle of still water and a half size bottle of Russian vodka. We started with hors d'oeuvres, then soup and a wonderful salad main course with an almost unending choice of meats and fish all beautifully prepared. A sweet came afterwards along with coffee and all the while, Russian white sparkling wine was freely flowing so by the end everyone was getting very drunk. One of our party filled his empty vodka bottle with water, pretending that it was vodka and challenged one of the Russian hosts to a drinking contest hoping that the Russian would become incapable. It appears that our Russian host was wise to this, as on a previous occasion whilst entertaining English guests, the same trick had been played on him. He grinned and said that as friends they should exchange gifts, picked up the vodka bottle containing the water and drank it down in one, leaving the real vodka to be drunk by our fellow traveller. About five minutes later our friend collapsed and was carried unconscious out of the room to be returned to the hotel prematurely by taxi. Our Russian host was most amused, roaring and laughing happily in the knowledge that he had managed this time to reverse the deception. After that, the party became a drunken and jolly affair with various Russians and English participants making frequent and silly speeches. I did spare a thought for the ordinary shabby Russians out there in the street, queuing at food shops often with little stock and realised that they would never see or even know that such opulence was there right under their noses in such a so-called equal society, or so they were told, controlled by the Communist Government.

I can't even remember what happened that evening but the next day we had to be ready for a conducted tour round the Kremlin which took all morning and the beginning of the afternoon. We had the rest of the afternoon free and after dinner at the hotel we were taken to The Kremlin Theatre to see a performance by The Bolshoi Ballet. Once again the ballet was beautiful and once again we were tired and I was ashamed again to be nodding off when I knew that I may never again get a chance to see the Bolshoi Ballet. I slept well that night ready for the next day which was to be my last full day in Russia.

I awoke to a beautiful sunny, warm day which was totally free to do as we wished. After breakfast a couple of us went out and ventured a little further afield and probably walked for a couple of miles. We eventually arrived in Red Square where an important event was obviously about to take place. The square itself was cordoned off and there were many television cameras on the sidelines ready to televise the forthcoming event. We waited for a while but nothing further seemed to be happening so we left, deciding to try out the Moscow Metro Underground System. The station was austere and blank but had ornate marble gothic pillars, a strange combination of austerity and grandeur. We got on a train but after four stops became nervous as all of the signs looked the same and decided if we lost count of the stops we may never get back to the correct station. Most ordinary Russians only understood their own language and we could not even read the sign of the station at which we boarded the train, so if we had got lost, getting back would have been virtually impossible. We therefore got out of the train and counted four stops back on our return journey safely arriving back to where we started. We made our way back to the hotel for dinner and were greeted by one of our party who invited us out to a restaurant to eat and drink whatever we wanted to be paid for by him. It turned out that he had done an enormous amount of black market money exchange transactions and had a great deal more money than he had receipts for. The value of goods that he had purchased just about balanced the value of his official money exchange receipts but if he had been found with even more Roubles on leaving the country, the game would have been up and he would have been in trouble. The only way that he could get rid of this money without trace was to buy food and drink, so we were all treated to a meal with lots of Russian fizzy wine. The food was mediocre, better than in the hotel but still not brilliant, but the wine was lovely.

By the time that we got out of the restaurant it was dark and I slowly started walking back to the hotel. Before long I was aware that I was being followed and when I reached a quiet spot in the shadows, I was stopped by a polite Russian young man who spoke perfect English. He asked me if he could buy my jacket as he liked western clothes as they were so much smarter than Russian ones. I told him that I did not want to sell my jacket but complimented him on his English. He said that conscription in Russia was compulsory and he had spent some time in the Russian navy where he had been to many countries, even the USA. Despite the Cold War it appeared that Russian ships did periodically put into American ports although it was never publicised at the time. He had become interested in the English language and had picked up much from whatever reading matter he could get hold of and also from the radio. I asked him what would happen if he got caught talking to me and trying to buy clothes and he said that it would result in about two hours' detention with a stern warning. I asked him what would happen if caught again and he said that for a second offence, one to two days' detention was usual. For a third offence however several months' imprisonment would follow but he told me that up to now he had never been caught. At that moment, two men wearing red armbands appeared from nowhere, each one grabbing an arm of his and they disappeared into thin air, leaving me standing in the dark and silence, absolutely alone and a little scared. I hurried back to the hotel, packed my things for our return journey back to England, then I went to bed.

First thing the next morning our bags had to be in the hotel lobby ready for loading on the coach but we had to keep them with us as we were all going to have our bags opened and searched by customs at Moscow Airport from where we were flying home. It was a blisteringly hot day and when we got to the airport I spent the remainder of my Russian money on a pot of caviar and half a bottle of vodka. There was a delay before our flight so we sat outside on a veranda sunbathing in the heat which had reached thirty one degrees centigrade, before eventually being called to Customs prior to boarding our plane. The officials were in a grim mood searching every nook and cranny of every case, not only checking our clothes but also our purchases and then examining all of our money exchange receipts. We definitely would not have got away with a serious amount of black market deals had we used the cash to buy gifts. Our passports were scrutinised and exit visas carefully examined at length, before being accepted by the officials who eventually directed us to board the aircraft standing nearby: a four engine propeller aircraft operated by Aeroflot.

We arrived back at Birmingham Airport late afternoon and up to now, I had not even thought about how I was going to get home.

I asked around to see if anyone was going north with whom I might scrounge a lift and one of our party from Blackburn suggested that he could hire a car and take me to Lancaster, dropping off another of our number on the way, if we could split the costs three ways. This seemed to be a perfect arrangement and worked well, getting me back to Lancaster in the early evening. I arrived home to complaints that I smelt like a Russian and was told to have a bath. I then remembered that a friend of mine who was a commercial traveller said that he had been to Russia once and everyone complained about how he smelled on his return.

When I had got myself sorted out, I found the caviar which I knew would not keep long and in the UK would have cost a fortune. My parents were unimpressed, however, and did not want any, so my sister and I ate it on cream crackers and thoroughly enjoyed it. At that time I was still smoking, as did my parents, and I had brought back some Russian cigarettes and decided to smoke one. My parents were still unimpressed and complained about the terrible smell that they imparted and asked me not to smoke them at home again. They were not big drinkers either so were not interested in the vodka, so I shared it with various friends who called on me, until it was eventually gone.

I had arrived back on a Saturday so was back at work the following Monday when I developed my black and white films and sent my colour slide films off for processing. Mr Robertson, Pat and Bill were all interested in my anecdotes but now it was time to get on with the usual day-to-day life of work once again. I soon had my photographs ready and put some on display in the shop for customers to see as many were very curious to find out how I had gone on in Russia. One of the most interested was Jean Robinson who had taught Fred, who, along with her parents and brother, had become even more regular customers. Jean asked me if I would give a slide show at her school about my time in Russia which I gladly did. The Footlights Club also asked me to give them the same slide show at one of their regular meetings so I also did this for them.

My ex-work colleague John Talbot had met a girl called Jane Cotching after he had moved south and they were to be married. John had asked me to be his best man but it meant that I would need to be away for the weekend at it was in Southborough near Tonbridge in Kent. John had arranged for us all to stay in a hotel nearby the night before but I had nowhere to stay on Saturday night after the wedding, prior to travelling home on Sunday. My friend Ken Ward once again obliged by smuggling me in and out of his accommodation as guests were still forbidden. We had met in the same local pub that we had frequented before and by the time I went back to Ken's place, I was pretty drunk, having also had plenty of alcohol at the wedding reception. The wedding had gone well and this time I know that I had done a much better job, as after the last experience, I knew what was expected of me and I had prepared myself properly for the task.

I had now changed my car as my old Ford Popular was causing problems and my dad had found an old Austin A30 car which I bought for £40. It had been hand painted pale blue in colour and looked a little untidy. I asked my dad if he could spray it fluorescent orange for me and after making enquiries as to the technique and paint required, he said that it would be possible. Shortly afterwards he and I together rubbed the entire car down with wet and dry paper to remove the previous hand painted coat of blue and to key the surface for the new paint. When my dad had finished it was amazing and glowed, especially in the half light. Most car colours were pretty drab then and my car shone like a beacon and everywhere I went, people were pointing at it as then it was absolutely unique.

My friend David Silver and I had still been going regularly to the cinema and drinking together at the Borough Club where we also played snooker, usually getting a game as they had two tables. We were often there on a Sunday night which was also ladies' night when wives, girlfriends and female relatives could also go and enjoy a drink with their menfolk. One of these was Carol Lofthouse whom I had previously met at Judith's Christmas party back in 1962. Her father was a club member so she and her mum used to come with her dad for the ladies' night on Sunday nights. Carol recognised me from Judith's party and also knew Dave slightly as her dad and David's dad were friends. When we were playing snooker she would often come and chat with us as there were few other members in our age group. One Sunday when I was not there, David asked Carol out and she agreed to be his regular girlfriend. I was pleased and astonished when I found out about the coincidence of this and that two people that I liked had found each other.

I suddenly did not see as much of Dave as I used to, as he was spending quite a lot of time with Carol but occasionally we were still going out for a drink and we did keep in touch frequently. Up to now I was still involved with the Footlights Club but my German lessons and bookkeeping studies had come to an end owing to the summer holidays. I had decided not to go back to German classes and to try and study more from home and I had now taken my GCE in bookkeeping which I ultimately passed, scraping through with a grade 'C'.

During the August Public holidays I fancied a trip to the north east so asked Dave and Carol if they were interested in coming too. At this time I had no girlfriend and had put all thoughts of such things on hold as I had still never found anyone that I had romantic feelings for, since losing my first love whilst still at school. Many of my friends were getting engaged or married and the amount of available girls of my age were diminishing as they were now getting snapped up. I asked my sister Marilyn if she would like to come along and she looked pleased to have been asked so off we went.

We called in at my cousin Ian's house first in Whitley Bay who looked astonished to see us. It turned out that earlier that morning, his mother, my Auntie Doris, had died in a house fire caused by her faulty electric blanket and he had rung the police in Lancaster, asking them to inform my parents. We had turned up two hours or so later having had no knowledge of this and at first he thought that we had come in response to his message and wondered how we could have arrived so quickly. Owing to the circumstances we did not stay long and carried on further north to Seahouses where we decided to find accommodation for the night. We got a meal and wandered around a little then decided to try and find somewhere to stay. Practically everyone had signs out saying 'No vacancies' until eventually we found a place with a 'Vacancies' sign. We knocked at the door but they only had one double room available so we booked Carol and Marilyn in and left them whilst Dave and I went looking for accommodation for ourselves. After a lot of searching and resigning ourselves to another night on the dunes sleeping in the car, we spotted a 'Vacancies' sign at 90 Main Street. The house had a porch on the front with a bell beside the door on the doorpost. I pressed the bell push which jammed in, ringing the bell continuously, despite my scrabbling with it to try and stop it ringing. The inner door abruptly opened and with the vibration the bell push popped out and the bell stopped ringing. A very angry looking lady opened the porch door and before we could speak verbally tore us apart for such inconsideration. Eventually when I got the opportunity to speak, I explained the situation and demonstrated the problem by activating the bell push which fortunately jammed again. Realising by now that it needed a vibration to stop it, I thumped the doorpost and it obligingly popped back out, proving my innocence. The lady then became very apologetic taking back all of the nasty comments that she had directed at us and asked what we wanted. I asked if she could put us up for the night pointing to the sign in her window. Her face fell as she explained that she had no room and had forgotten to reverse the sign to say 'No vacancies'. She must have seen the look on our faces and after the tongue lashing that we had endured, took pity on us, offering us the bed settee in her front room if we did not mind waiting until all of her other guests had retired to bed. We said that we did not mind and went off to collect the girls, grab some food and spend an evening in The Ship Hotel near the harbour. Eventually we left, the girls going to their place and us making our way down Main Street where there was a hot drink and biscuits waiting for us.

We had a very comfortable night on the bed settee and awoke the next morning to a sea fret, or haar as it is sometimes called, but whatever its name is, you could hardly see your hand in front of your face. We were given a superbly cooked substantial breakfast and by now were getting along very well with our host and hostess, a couple called Ann and Bart Whillis. I asked Ann if we came this way again could we book our stay and she said that would be fine, giving us her telephone number so that we could ring in advance of any future visits. She also charged us a reduced rate owing to the fact we had to sleep on the bed settee.

We picked up the girls, who had also had a comfortable night, but I think that their breakfast had not been as generous as ours. We decided not to hang around near the coast but to head inland in the hope that the visibility would improve. We made our way to Alnwick and then on to Rothbury and all of the while, the visibility did improve until eventually were found ourselves in bright sunshine. We wandered around Rothbury and had lunch there before driving home. On arrival back at our house, my mother was most relieved to see us, as shortly after we had set off from home, a policeman had arrived at the door telling her that he had some bad news to impart and her first thought was that we had all been killed in a road accident. She said that it came almost as a relief to find that it had been my Auntie Doris and not us but after she had time to gather her thoughts, she was so ashamed of her feelings. However, I know that is a natural reaction, now having children of my own.

At work Mr Robertson had arranged with Kodak for me to go on a managerial course which was from a Monday to Friday and took place in their Kingsway headquarters in London. It turned out to be in the same building and the same room where I had been in 1964 doing my Kodak sales course. All of the candidates stayed in a small hotel in Bayswater called the 'Kings Court' which was a strange hotel with even more strange goings on.

As residents, we were all looking forward to the possibility of sitting in the bar and going to bed when we were ready at a time not necessarily regulated by licensing hours. On the Monday night we were all in bed pretty early but on Tuesday night we were in the bar which closed at ten thirty despite our protests that we were residents. The management were unsympathetic and said that staff were not available to man the bar indefinitely, so it always closed at ten thirty pm. On the Wednesday night we overcame that problem by stocking up on sufficient drinks before the bar closed, to keep up going for a couple of hours after closing time. Whilst sitting there, we soon realised why the management had tried to discourage us from hanging around, when a slow but steady stream of couples kept walking through the bar area to the back of the hotel, returning and leaving a little while later. Shortly afterwards some of the same girls were going through again but each time with a different man. It did not take a lot of imagination to realise that this was a 'Knocking Shop' and by making some ground floor rooms available and the bar empty, up to now they had been getting away with this lucrative sideline. The next day we advised Kodak of our findings as they had recommended and booked this hotel for us. They said that they were shocked and would in future use somewhere else.

Mr Robertson was getting close to retirement age and on

November 8th he was sixty five years old. With five and a half years' experience under my belt plus the completion of my apprenticeship, various educational visits and courses attended, along with looking after the shop during his absences, he made it known that he would wind down gradually and give me greater responsibility. I was still going to his house every Monday evening to do the books but now not just to learn but to take some weight off his shoulders. We were both working on different books making the working evening shorter that it used to be. Mrs Robertson was still spoiling me by giving me all of my favourite things for tea and I now knew her so well that I used to tease her with outrageous comments and she was no longer saying 'He is only a child'.

Saturday December 7th was a normal fairly busy pre-Christmas day. All of our decorations were up at the shop and the Christmas windows had been dressed about two weeks previously. Late in the afternoon, Mrs Robertson had come in, having done some shopping in town, and as often happened now on a Saturday, Mr Robertson said, 'Well, I'm off now, lock up at half past five, have a good weekend and I'll see you on Monday morning' and he left the shop along with Mrs Robertson. Sunday December 8th was a day that I will never forget, as it was the day which was set to decide the whole future of my life. It was a gloomy December day with a chill in the air but not bitterly cold. During the afternoon, I had decided to go to Williamson's Park where there was going to be a happening, a hippy sort of event with people wandering around in flowing clothes and painted faces. I took my camera loaded with colour transparency film as I expected plenty of photo opportunities, which there were and I got lots of good pictures. Williamson's Park had a large, imposing domed monument and the door of the monument building was closed but when I turned the handle it opened and I went inside and closed the door behind me. I had been in there plenty of times before but usually in the summer months when it was officially open to visitors, so I knew my way around pretty well. Visitors were permitted to go up to the second level which had an outside balcony just below the copper dome. In the past I had spotted a door in the wall which had always been locked but today when I tried it, the door opened. I had always suspected that it was the entrance to a staircase taking you to a small building right on top of the dome and when I went inside I indeed found a wide metal spiral staircase which took me right to the top. At the top there was a short wooden ladder leading to a trapdoor which when I pushed popped open and I was now right on top of the dome. I stood in there for a while knowing that I should not be there but it had been a lifetime's ambition to stand here and get what is probably the best possible view looking over Lancaster. After about five minutes, I heard a sound and quickly descended in case I got caught or even worse got locked in. I don't know what caused the sound but I came downstairs and let myself out of the structure with the satisfaction that I had not been caught and was one of the few people ever to get right to the very top of the Williamson's Park Memorial.

I went home and had my tea and cannot remember what else I did during the evening but did not go to bed very early that night. I often used to sit in our front room which I had decorated for my parents earlier in the year and as it was to my taste, I often used to sit in there to play records or listen to the radio. Shortly after midnight there was an urgent knock on the door and when I opened it, a young man called David Currie was stood there. Bill Cowell by now was no longer working for us and David had been his short term replacement, although he had also recently left us to work as a photographer for one of the local newspapers. David had just witnessed a road accident in the Lancaster Town Centre, where the driver in the car in front of him had collapsed and died at the wheel of his car, which had then slowly drifted across the road knocking down a pedestrian. David had got out of his car to see if there was anything he could do and recognised the driver who had died as being Mr Robertson. He had tried to comfort Mrs Robertson as best as possible but shortly afterwards she had been taken away by the police and he had come straight round to our house as he thought that I should know immediately what had happened. I was shaken, in shock and did not know what to do, my mind was in a whirl and I could not think straight. I decided to go to bed and make sure that I got down to the shop early the next morning to await further news but I did not sleep well and was down at the shop in good time, not really knowing what was going to happen next.

On Monday December 9th at about nine thirty, Mrs McCormack, Mr Robertson's sister-in-law, came into the shop and told me to close up and go home. I said that this sounded a little extreme as I could manage and if she could get her hands on the books and bring them in, I could keep things going until more rational decisions could be made. Mrs Robertson's nephew, who was an accountant for a large company, seemed to be making the interim decisions and I got a message back to keep the shop open and running as usual and he would call and see me at home the following Sunday. The shop's bank account had been closed but a new temporary one had been opened to allow the shop's takings after Mr Robertson's death to be banked. I wrote to all of the companies who provided our stock to inform them of the situation and promised them that they would be paid in due course after the affairs were all sorted out and without exception they all continued to provide us with stock. The books were given to me on Sunday 15th December after I had a long chat with Mrs Robertson's nephew and satisfied him that I could cope. Pat had been off ill at the beginning of the week but had returned later in the week so there were at least two of us to deal with the busy time just before Christmas. I was not allowed by the family to see Mrs Robertson for a few days as she was extremely upset, in a state of deep shock and had been taken to her sister's house where she still was and owing to her state of mind remained there for about three months. When she saw me she wept continuously and it was not possible at this stage to discuss any business matters with her, but after trying to comfort her as best I could, I said that I would go back to see her every week and keep in touch. I got the feeling that her sister did not welcome my visit as I was not family and I was given the impression that I was considered to be interfering although nothing like that was ever said. The funeral came shortly afterwards and I closed the shop for the whole of that day as a mark of respect, despite it being so close to Christmas. The service was held at Hest Bank Church and I was surprised how few people attended considering that Mr Robertson was very well known and had been a prominent member of the Lancaster Golf Club for many years. After the church service the family went on to the crematorium for the committal but it was made very clear to me that I would not be welcome at this part of the service, as it was for family only. I discovered later that Mr Robertson's ashes were interred at St. Paul's Church, Lancaster in a newly appointed area for that purpose and his name was included in a memorial book kept inside the church. Every year on the anniversary of his death, the book is opened at the page recording it, so anyone can still see the memorial text if they choose to go and see it at the appropriate time.

The customer reaction was quite strange – all were sympathetic and most I continued to serve but I noticed that a few had disappeared who had obviously preferred Mr Robertson or wanted the attention of the shop proprietor. They had obviously defected to our competitors Cecil Thomas Ltd, a short distance away, where they still could have that type of attention. I knew that the only way to recapture that type of business was to own the business and to age about twenty years, as the odd older customer did not like taking the advice of a twenty two year old should they need help.

Christmas that year was so full of distractions and most of my friends were in one way or another tied up with their women so I probably didn't do a lot of visiting but spent more time that previously at home; however, I don't really remember as my life was so tied up with the business which had now become my first priority. Hogmanay would have been spent at Brian's parents' house as this Scottish type of celebration was something that I always enjoyed, although the way that events worked out the following year, it was to be my last one with Brian's parents.

1969

I was now living in very uncertain times as at the beginning of the year, I did not know whether or not the business would remain as it was or be sold. I did not know if I would even have future employment but I kept buying and selling stock and continued to keep the books up to date. The business had been issued with new cheque books but I did not have authority to sign cheques so on my weekly visits to see Mrs Robertson, she had to sign cheques for our wages and in due course to settle our outstanding debts with suppliers, which all went perfectly to plan. Lots of well-wishers concerned for my future popped into the shop and wanted to know what was happening but at this point I could not tell them; I was nevertheless touched by the goodwill shown to me.

Once again I was contacted by Mr Wilkes, this time to take a class in Halton, otherwise to do exactly the same as the previous year. This I did although towards the end of the course I introduced some lighting and darkroom demonstrations as the pupils on this course were a little more advanced than the ones that I had taught the previous year.

Half way through March, I was summoned to go and see the shop's accountant, a man called Mr Dalton. A meeting had been arranged with him, along with Mrs Robertson and her solicitor, Mr Swainson. After previous meetings that had apparently taken place as to the future of the business, it had been decided to offer me a partnership by giving me one eighth of the business and using the income of that to purchase a further one eighth over a period of five years so that by 1974 I would own a one quarter share of the value of the business. They had done this to ensure that I would continue to have employment, would not walk away and give the business the dedication and time that it required to maintain its success. As I would be drawing a share of the profits to pay for my one eighth, Mrs Robertson would draw her equivalent larger share to give her an income. My salary was a separate entity but was enhanced to reflect my position in the business and the responsibility that I was taking on. The solicitor and accountant had recognised that this was the only way forward as I had no savings or independent income and could not have become a partner in any other way.

Since Bill Cowell had left, we had employed one or two assistants who had not stayed for long and once again we needed another employee. There were a few applicants but one who stood out was a youth called Keith Duffy. I knew Keith and his older brother Philip through the Footlights club as they were both keen on amateur dramatics and had no hesitation in employing him because I knew that he was honest and reliable. In the early days, I had realised that holidays and time off were going to be a problem as Pat did not deal with complicated sales and Keith had no experience, so I resigned myself to having no holiday leave for the time being. My social life had been scaled down owing to the time that I was spending looking after the business but I always went out on Saturday night to meet up with my friends at a modern town centre pub called The Lancastrian. Quite a gang of us used to gather there every week and we all knew that if we went in on a Saturday night there would be plenty of familiar faces so this was now

171

my regular haunt on a Saturday night. Just across the street was a chip shop called 'The Star Supper Bar' run by its proprietor called Jack. We would leave the pub shortly before last orders and go into The Star for a sit down supper of fish and chips shortly before they finished for the night but greatly to the consternation of their washing up lady, Mrs Thompson, who always complained that she had just finished her chores for the night when our gang descended. With a few pints of beer inside us, we used to joke with her and one evening offered to wash up after we had finished the meal. She laughed and didn't take us seriously but when our plates were empty we filled the sink full of water and washing up liquid, then washed and dried all of the pots ourselves. Every Saturday after that we always did the same but Mrs Thompson never got home any earlier as she would sit and laugh at us whilst we washed the pots and teased her. On a Sunday night I still often used to go into The Borough where Dave and Carol, along with their parents, would be, and Dave and I would have a game of snooker.

One morning an envelope arrived for me and it was an invitation to the wedding of Miss Judith Hodgson and Mr David Jackman. Over the last couple of years or so, Judith and I had gone our separate ways and I had hardly seen her. I did not recognise the name of her prospective husband as it was not the person that she had been going out with after she had told me she was seeing someone three years previously and I did not realise that she had found someone else in the meantime. The wedding was to take place on a Saturday which meant that I could not go owing to my commitments at the shop and I was bitterly disappointed. Owing to the high regard that I had for Judith, I was happy that she had found someone to share her life with but felt that I was going to let her down terribly by not attending her wedding. Rather than write, I decided to pop down to her house to explain. When I arrived, her mum opened the door and asked me in. It seemed that Judith had been in the bath and appeared moments later dressed in a bath robe. Her mum then tried to usher her out of the room but Judith told her mum not to be so silly as she was perfectly decent and fully covered up. I explained to them both that I was so really sorry that I could not be at the wedding and explained why. Judith was fine about it and expressed her regret that I wouldn't be there so I wished her the very best of luck for the future, gave her a peck on the cheek and left.

A month or two went by and I had now settled down into the routine of running the shop and the staff situation was now working well. I had no evening classes and the Footlights did not meet much during midsummer so my social life was not as hectic as it had been previously. However, I had been thinking a lot about Jean Robinson (Fred's ex-teacher), could not get her out of my mind. I resolved that next time she came into the shop that I would ask her out and warned Pat of what I was going to do so that Pat could make herself scarce when Jean came in. It did not take long and on Monday 30th June, Jean called in at lunchtime and Pat disappeared. I cannot remember what Jean came in to buy but after she had made her purchase I asked her if she was free the following evening to come out with me and she said that she would like that. I said that I would pick her up in my car and take her home at the end of the evening so transport would not be an issue. Dave Silver only worked a few doors away from me as he was still a gents' hairdresser for Maison Knowles, so I popped along to see him and told him what was happening to see if he and Carol could join us to make up a foursome, as I thought it would take away some of the awkwardness of a first date. He said that was possible and I arranged to pick him and Carol up in Lancaster after I had picked up Jean at Arkholme.

On July 1st, I could not concentrate on anything except the forthcoming evening which I was so looking forward to. Eventually it came and I arrived promptly at Jean's house called 'Thorneys' at

Arkholme to take her out. She invited me into her house where and her family greeted me full of smiles so I immediately felt that I had been given the seal of approval. Shortly afterwards we set off for Lancaster, I explained to Jean that I had arranged with Dave for us to go out in a foursome and hoped that she did not mind. She said that she was completely happy with that and shortly afterwards we were in Lancaster where I picked up Dave and Carol and introduced them to Jean. It was a beautiful sunny evening and we ended up at Heysham, going to the Strawberry Gardens Pub for a drink. I parked the car and as Jean and I were walking along to the pub our hands touched and we spontaneously held hands as we walked along. We settled down in the pub for a relaxed evening and chatted away with everyone getting along really well together and the evening passed quickly. We returned to Lancaster where I dropped Dave and Carol off and then continued back to Arkholme with a warm glow inside and the girl that I was starting to love sitting next to me. I did not feel in the least bit awkward and the conversation flowed easily between us and after a few minutes we were back at Arkholme. I had not intended to ask Jean out again for a week or two but I could no longer help myself and asked her if she would like to go out again on Friday, in three days' time, to which she agreed. We kissed goodnight and I drove home back to Lancaster having already fallen in love.

Friday could not come quickly enough and when it did I eagerly made my way to Arkholme in time for our second date. Jean asked me if I would like to look around where she lived, as the house was next to a market garden containing lots of greenhouses as well as having its own extensive garden, flowerbeds and outbuildings. She showed me around everywhere and I quickly gleaned that she was passionate about gardening as she explained that was what the family did for a living, with her father and aunt growing tomatoes in the greenhouses helped by her mother. She also explained that during busy times she was expected to help, particularly picking tomatoes as when they are ripe there is only a small timescale in which they can be picked, packed and sent to market and often the amount ripening at the same time was more than just her parents and aunt could cope with. I said that if extra hands were needed I would be willing to learn but that offer was turned down as the tomatoes had to be picked quickly, carefully and in a very particular way which needed experience.

After spending about half an hour looking around we went off in the car, I think to the cinema at Lancaster as I had continued to do my cinema photography and was still getting free tickets. I took Jean home at the end of the evening and again kissed her goodnight and asked if she would like to go out on Sunday afternoon and she said that she would and to call for her at about two thirty in the afternoon.

Sunday was not far away and it soon came around and I eagerly arrived as arranged, to be met by her brother Peter who said that she was not well and was in bed but I could come in and wait as she would be getting up later. I was devastated – was this an excuse, did she have afterthoughts? All of these questions were going on in my mind and I thought that I was losing her. I sat and watched television whilst I waited and about an hour later Jean appeared, looking a little washed out. I think that she had asked Peter to leave us alone as suddenly we had privacy and Jean explained that she really had felt unwell but was a little better now. Jean said to me that she had been so worried that I might think it was an excuse to get out of our date but nothing could be further from the truth and she was glad that I had waited until she had felt better. I was elated as I now knew that she had really wanted to go out with me and that she too was worried that I might have rejected her. I seem to remember that owing to the circumstances we did not go out but I was invited for tea which her mum, along with Jean, helped prepare. I quickly realised that these ladies could cook as my tea was delicious and although Jean already had my heart she

175

had it all over again with the saying that 'The quickest way to a man's heart is through his stomach'!

I always did my bookkeeping on a Monday night so did not go out with her then but on Tuesday I went over to Arkholme and with Jean's guidance drove around a lot of the local country lanes which at that time I did not know. It was a sunny evening and we were enjoying each other's company so much that in no time at all, we were back at Thorneys and it was time for me to go home. Later in the week, Jean and I were out in Lancaster and when we got back into the car, I could contain myself no longer and told her of my feelings despite only having been together for a few days. To my relief she said that she felt the same about me and we kissed then set off back for Arkholme.

One minor distraction to everyone was the very first moon landing which took place on 20th July. Marilyn and I stayed up practically all night watching television to catch the first pictures transmitted back showing the first moon walk. It turned out that Jean and her family had done the same as had practically the whole country and the following day there were many tired people walking around.

As Jean worked in Lancaster we started meeting in our lunch hours when they coincided. This was not every day as Jean had to do some dinner duties at school and occasionally I would have a customer who kept me from having my lunch on time. I went over to Arkholme several evenings a week which meant that Jean and I were seeing each other practically every day until the school holidays started. During August her grandmother on her mother's side of the family died, so Jean, along with some of her family, had to go to Tilehurst near Reading where her grandmother had lived and where the funeral was being held. Although at this stage Jean did not drive, she was learning and owned a beige Morris Mini which she had bought new via a loan from her dad which she was repaying monthly. This was considerably more reliable than my old bright orange Austin A30 which by now had the nickname as the Orange Bomb, so the family travelled in Jean's car driven by her brother Peter who had already passed his test. They were due to return a few days later when I heard that there had been an accident on the return journey resulting in them all ending up in hospital at Cirencester. I had never known anyone so close to me being in that situation before and I was worried to an extent that I had never been before. I later heard that everyone basically was ok except for Peter who had facial injuries resulting in a lot of stitches and although disfiguring and inconvenient, it fortunately was not life threatening.

They eventually returned and I was relieved to see that Jean was physically fine although very shaken and a little more distant than she had been. She and Peter were always quite close and I think that she was still very worried about his eventual recovery and to what extent that his injuries would show. Her car had been very badly damaged although not written off and after a few weeks it was returned to them after having been repaired. Eventually the shock wore off and life for us got back to normal but it was quite a long time before Peter's face healed properly and his scars went away.

Holidays at the shop were very difficult for me now but I engineered four days' leave at the end of August by taking just the bank holiday Tuesday off. The shop never opened on Wednesdays so by taking just this one day, it combined Sunday to Wednesday to give me the four days that I wanted. I was dying to take Jean up to the north east and arranged for us to stay with Mary on the Sunday night. I then rang Ann Whillis in Seahouses to see if she could do Bed and Breakfast for us on the Monday night, taking a chance that we would find something on Tuesday night on the way back home. The reason for that was Jean's cousin Robin who lived in Stonehaugh worked in the Wark forest as a foreman forester and she wanted to look him up on the way back and introduce me to him and his wife Judith, so to stay nearby on Tuesday night seemed like a good idea.

I had told Jean so much about the rugged beauty of Northumberland and how quiet the beaches were that I now wanted her to experience them and hoped that they would thrill her as much as they did me. We set off on Sunday morning and meandered up to the north east via Hexham and carried on until we eventually arrived to stay with Mary and her son, my second cousin Philip, who was a quiet boy, in Whitley Bay. She and Jean seemed to get on well although I found out later that she thought her to be quite shy and next to me it probably seemed that way as I am a fairly gregarious person with people that I know well.

On Monday we made our way to Morpeth to see my Auntie Phyllis. My aunt had been a long term patient at St. George's Mental Institution and was the sister of my dad, my Uncle Archie and my Auntie Doris. I had only found out about her a couple of years earlier as she was a family embarrassment and nobody talked about her or visited her. Apparently as a girl she had a strong personality and after being injured in collision with a cyclist at the age of twelve, her parents had given in to her every whim making her difficult to deal with. The story goes that my grandfather before his death made my Uncle Archie and his wife Dora promise to look after her, give her a home and in return he left his house to them. Shortly after the death of my grandfather, my uncle and aunt had Phyllis dumped in St. Georges and the rest is history. This was the reason why my father hated his sister-in-law, as he blamed her for talking my uncle into doing this deed. I had been horrified to learn that no one had visited her in twenty years including my father, so had vowed that I would do so every time that I visited the north east and always did so until her death in 1982. Right from the start I had told Jean of my Auntie Phyllis and she supported me, always being with me when I visited her starting now. Unfortunately Auntie Phyllis was developing dementia so she had difficulty in realising who I was but nevertheless I felt duty bound to visit her when I could and although she never knew precisely who I was, she did realise that I was a member of her family.

After leaving Morpeth we made our way to Seahouses, first unloading our belongings at Ann's house. Ann had remembered me from last year owing to the bell incident and having to put Dave and myself up on her bed settee. Jean and I had a room each as respectable unmarried couples then would never sleep together in holiday accommodation but we weren't doing that anyway. We then went out and I took Jean straight down to the beach and sand dunes between Seahouses and Bamburgh where we parked the car and made our way through the dunes onto a deserted stretch of sands about two miles long and then we were alone. This was heaven as I strolled along hand in hand with Jean, appreciating life and how very lucky that I was. We eventually made our way back to Seahouses where we left the car near Ann's house and got fish and chips at a chip shop called 'Moles' near the harbour. We then went into the Ship Hotel to a bar called the 'Captain's Cabin', where we had a couple of drinks. Before returning to Ann's for the night we walked to the end of the harbour and stood behind the harbour light where we could see the Longstone Lighthouse, eventually walking back to retire for the night. By the time that we got back to Ann's house, her husband Bart had returned from work and having met him the previous year, I was soon chatting but Jean was silent. Ann said that she would get tea and biscuits for supper and Bart left the room with her. Jean looked at me and apologised for not speaking to him owing to the fact that she had not understood a word that he had said, with his very strong Northumbrian accent. I had never thought about it before but being used to my relatives and having spent a long holiday nearby when eight years old, I was accustomed to the accent and never realised that people who had never heard it before had great difficulty at first, in understanding it.

The following morning after breakfast we took the car back to the dunes and decided to go into the sea. Each of us got changed behind a different sand dune, me emerging in my swimming trunks and Jean in a bikini. This was the first time that I had seen her wearing so little; she looked stunning in her bikini and I could hardly keep my eyes off her. Once again the beach was completely empty so that we had it all to ourselves and I was enchanted by this lovely bikini-clad girl with whom I was intensely in love. The North Sea, however, is very chilly at any time of the year and after a few minutes we were both very cold so it was back behind our respective dunes where a few minutes later we emerged fully clad. We had quite a lot of the day left so travelled on to Eyemouth and then St. Abbs, both just over the border in Scotland. I had never driven those extra few miles north before, the weather was good and we enjoyed both places but I was on a high just being with Jean on our first holiday together.

We had to think about where we were going to stay for this last evening and decided that Rothbury would be a good spot and made our way there although it was dark when we arrived. We found a house offering bed and breakfast and asked the lady who answered the door if she had two rooms free. She said that she did with a beaming smile, as she realised that by ordering a room each we were respectable and were quickly shown to our rooms and went straight to bed as it was getting quite late but sneaking a goodnight kiss on the landing before we retired. After breakfast the next day we started looking for Stonehaugh but had initially got mixed up with Greenhough so arrived there first. After realising our mistake we did eventually get to Stonehaugh, which was some distance away from Greenhough, but Jean's cousin and his wife were out. We went to Wark for lunch and tried later back at Stonehaugh but as far as I can remember don't think that we met them on that occasion. After that we drove straight home dropping Jean off first at Thorneys and then back to Lancaster for me, as I was back at work on the Thursday.

Our first holiday together had been a huge success, we had got on so well together and I loved Jean more and more as time went on. We both seemed to like many of the same things and I could almost mind read what she was thinking as she could with me. We were obviously very compatible and I wanted to be with Jean for the rest of my life so it was now time to propose to her. On the 10th September, I had spent the evening at Thorneys when Jean and I were left in their television room for a few moments on our own. She came and sat on my knee and I could not contain myself any longer and asked her to marry me. Without hesitation she smiled, said yes and we hugged and kissed each other before anyone else came back into the room. I suggested that we should keep it a secret for a day or two until I had asked her father's permission which I did the following evening and he said straight away that I could marry his daughter. Although we told our families immediately, we decided not to announce our engagement officially until the middle of October when Jean was on holiday from school. We were going away again, this time to London and put an engagement announcement in the local paper so all of our friends found out at the same time and as not to show anyone favour. I also needed to organise buying Jean an engagement ring so we went looking in Lancaster and Jean eventually found one that she liked. I had forty pounds in the bank and fortunately the ring cost thirty six so I could afford the one that she chose. After we bought it she said that she had been worried that what she liked might be too expensive but I assured her that although there was only four pounds left, I would have spent my last penny on her but now we would both have to save to afford to set up home together. She said that she would like to also buy something for me and chose a beautiful set of sterling silver cuff links which I still use and cherish to this day.

After the 10th September Jean and I spent alternate weekends staying at each other's houses. When in Lancaster we spent Saturday nights at the Lancastrian Pub and Jean became a firm fixture amongst my circle of friends. From being a young boy I had always attended the Presbyterian Church on Queen Street, Lancaster and on Jean's weekends in Lancaster, she always came with me to church. In Arkholme, Jean's dad was a church warden at the C of E church there so when I stayed in Arkholme, we both went to the services there. Up to now our parents had not met each other so my parents invited Jean's mum and dad to come over to Portland Street for an early supper and an introductory chat one evening. Jean came along with them but shortly after they arrived, Jean and I went out, leaving them to it, as we thought that without our presence, they would all have to talk to each other. On our return all seemed well as they had found some common ground in mutual acquaintances and were comparing notes rather that discussing us or our forthcoming marriage. Our mums got on particularly well together and did in fact remain the very best of friends until my mum eventually died in 2009.

Mrs Robertson had returned home during the late spring but was still in a very delicate state. She and her sister had kept falling out so she decided that there was no alternative but to go home and make the best of things. I no longer went on Monday nights but she had started coming into the shop fairly frequently to sign cheques as these had now to bear both of our signatures. When she heard that I had found a girlfriend and was getting engaged she was most worried, mainly that it would distract me from the business but after she had met Jean, she seemed much calmer about the situation and as time went on became very fond of her. Mrs Robertson and I did, in fact, become very close – she was the granny that after six years old I never had and she treated me almost like the son that she never had.

During the October break from School, I took two or three days off work so Jean and I could go to London to stay with John Talbot and his wife Jane as they had invited us for a visit. Jean had never met them before but immediately got along with them really well. They lived at 44 Trinity Church Square, Southwark, which was close to a main road and although we slept reasonably well on our first night, the traffic roaring past after about six thirty the next morning was so deafening, we had to get up. Jean slept in their spare bedroom and I slept on the settee as Jean and I, despite our love for each other, were still not in a sexual relationship. As John and Jane were mostly at work we had to entertain ourselves and owing to Jean's fondness of gardening we spent a lot of our time going round Kew Gardens which Jean adored. By now I knew my way pretty well around central London so we did manage to fit in a little sightseeing but Kew Gardens occupied the majority of our time.

By the time that we got home, all of our friends knew that we were engaged and had been so shocked that I, being a confirmed bachelor in June, had fallen in love and was engaged to be married by October. They did not realise that we had actually decided to marry early in September and had declared our love for each other within about ten days of our first date. There were loads of congratulation cards waiting for us and so many joyous messages of support from friends, neighbours and Jean's work colleagues; we were overwhelmed by the love shown to us by everyone who knew us. Many of Jean's work colleagues had been my teachers at Dallas Road School so they were particularly pleased, and owing to the circumstances, several of these ex-teachers of mine were now becoming my personal friends.

We were now moving towards Christmas and this one was going to be very different to the last few years with Jean by my side, now almost inseparable, so we had to make time for our respective families but wanted to be together. We did this by us each having Christmas dinner with our own families but with me going to Jean's house in the evening. I think that on Boxing Day we spent much of it together but sharing our time between both of our families. I cannot remember what we did on New Year's Eve but whatever we did do, we did it together.

1970

I have very little recollection of early days in this year but the lives of Jean and I revolved around each other and much of my time was spent at Arkholme when we were not in Lancaster or Morecambe, going to the cinema or other distractions previously described. I had now deserted the Footlights club although I did occasionally see some of the friends that I had made socially. Early in the year wedding plans had not started in earnest although I think that the actual date had been set and the church booked. Unusually for that time, the wedding was not going to be on a Saturday but on a Wednesday, to coincide with our closing day at the shop which meant that I could get about ten days' holiday afterwards by having only one Saturday off work, Saturday always being a very busy day. Jean wanted August 12th, 'The glorious twelfth', the first day of the Grouse shooting season. She was not into shooting or anything like that but confessed years later to me it was because of the failings in my memory and so much fuss always being made prior to the twelfth about Grouse shooting, that I would never forget our wedding anniversary and she was right, I never have!

We had to address where we were going to live when we were married and Jean's dad offered us Rose Cottage, which he had owned for the previous fourteen years to accommodate workers at the gardens when he used to employ outside labour. It was eventually to be used for Jean's parents' retirement but he said that we could live there until that time came. A young, newly married local couple were living there at first but knew that it was a short term let until Jean was married so they moved out shortly before we were due to move in.

As winter went away and springtime took over, wedding fever increased and Jean was choosing bridesmaids. This had to be done in good time as all of the dresses including the bride's dress were being made by Jean's mother with a little assistance by Jean. There were five bridesmaids, Jean's sister Joan, my sister Marilyn, Jean's best friend Dorothy Skitt, Jean's cousin Valerie and Jean's second cousin Tracy, then only about seven years old. During this time I got to know Jean's brother Peter a little better as both of us had to keep out of the way much of the time as the women got on with wedding plans and dressmaking. Peter was very practical, being keen on building and repairing things. He fitted a lawnmower engine to a homemade go-kart and used to scoot around the gardens at great speed on this contraption which nowadays would probably break every health and safety rule in existence. We did in fact share many of the same interests so I enjoyed immensely the times that we found ourselves in each other's company. Peter was still at school studying for his A Level examinations so was also very busy with his schoolwork. He came home one day having been in serious trouble at school, having tried out an unofficial chemistry experiment that went wrong. He and a few friends had got the correct mix of chemicals to make nitroglycerine, a highly unstable explosive that can blow up, even by just mixing the component chemicals together. I gather that they thought if they only put a single drop of each component into a vessel that would be safe even if anything went wrong, owing to the extremely small quantity involved. They were wrong as when the final component was included there was a terrific explosion blowing the door off the locker in which they were mixing the experiment and leaving Peter deaf in one ear. The noise was so loud that it was heard throughout the whole school and the game was up. Peter and his friends were in serious trouble and reprimanded but I think that they got away lightly as the teaching staff were so relieved that the situation was not far worse. Had they not taken the precautions that they did and tried to mix more, they could have been killed and blown the side off the school building!

One day I got a telephone call at work from my friend David Rack in Stoke-on-Trent. Despite Dave being one of my best friends he never usually rang me so I wondered what was happening. He told me that Mrs Teale, his granny, had died whilst staying with them and that I should know, although he had waited until after the funeral had taken place, as he knew that I would have gone to it and thought that there was no point in travelling all that way just to attend a funeral. I was very upset as I dearly loved that old lady and whilst David put a brave front on and remained very matter of fact about the situation, I knew that he must have been upset also, as he loved his granny more than anyone else in the world. She was eighty six years old and a wonderful old lady, often telling fibs to our parents to get David and me out of scrapes when we were children. She was and still is the oldest person that I have ever known who was so young at heart and mixed so well with and was loved by youngsters two generations younger than herself.

By the time that summer started, wedding invitations were sent out and I had to supply a list of my relations, friends and anyone connected to me that had to be invited to the wedding. The banns were soon to be called in church so Jean and I were invited to the vicar's house for a chat. After some preliminary preambling, the vicar asked me in which parish I lived in Lancaster. I told him that I did not know as the parish boundary had been moved by only one row of houses a few weeks previously and I did not know whether 45 Portland Street was in the new parish or one more row deeper into the old parish, as the old parish boundary had gone down the middle of the street leaving each side in a different parish. The change had been made so that the whole of Portland Street was in the same parish but I did not know which way the line had been moved but I would find out. At this the vicar completely lost his temper, shouted at me and said that I had no right to come and visit him so ill prepared with inadequate information. Although I have a long fuse, I was astonished at his attitude and also lost my temper, pointing out to him that I had been a regular churchgoer since the age of two years old, had never missed a single Sunday School class from the age of ten to fifteen years old and was still going to church practically every week, albeit the Presbyterian Church. How could he expect me, a Presbyterian, to anticipate the peculiarities of the Church of England or realise how important that this question would be? I had offered to find the answer quickly and could not see why he should be so upset. We had got off to a very bad start which had caused mutual wounds that never really healed and after that time neither of us were ever comfortable in each other's company again. Before we left, however, he composed himself, probably realising that he had never given us the usual advice pointing out that marriage is sacred, for life and for the procreation of children. He still never gave us that advice but on leaving touched my arm and said, 'Be gentle, be gentle'. We walked back to Jean's parents' house and after the shock had worn off about his outburst, Jean and I started giggling at his final comments about being gentle.

Earlier in the year during Jean's February break at school, we had gone to stay with her cousin Robin and his wife Judith, in the Wark Forest, after the failed attempt at meeting them the previous October. It had been bitterly cold with snow on the ground and after their invitation, Judith's mum had turned up. The sleeping arrangements had been very makeshift but I got the best out of it by sleeping on the settee in front of a lovely open fire, so was as warm as toast. Everyone else in other parts of the house were frozen stiff and sleeping in several layers of clothes. Robin had taken us out for a whole day on the forestry roads, which were interesting and picturesque, but we were chilled to the bone by the time that we got back before darkness fell. He invited us to return when the weather was better so during the May Bank Holidays, we went for another visit. The weather was very hot for the time of the year so the house was comfortably warm and this time Judith's mum was not there so Robin put Jean and me in his spare room containing a double bed, not realising that, as yet, we had never slept together. Nothing was said to him, so for the first time, we found ourselves in this situation not entirely of our making and did sleep together. I am not prepared to elaborate any further except to say that we had a wonderful night and found ourselves even more in love with each other than ever before.

The shop continued to be busy but one minor complication had occurred in that Pat was pregnant and would be leaving soon. Keith, however, was by now becoming very experienced and I knew that it would be possible to leave him with a new member of staff to hold the fort whilst Jean and I were on our honeymoon. Mrs Robertson would also be popping in frequently and although she could not do anything, her very presence would keep the staff on their toes and ensure that everything would be ok.

One evening in Arkholme, I was with Jean at Thorneys when the most violent thunderstorm broke out and was coming our way. Jean started pulling plugs out of sockets in case of a lightning strike when, without warning, there was a huge bang and a gigantic spark came straight out of a socket from which Jean had just removed a plug. Despite her being about three feet away, it hit her in the hand holding the plug and threw her across the room in my direction. She came towards me at such speed flying through the air that there was no hope that I could catch her completely but I did manage to catch her head as her body dropped to the ground and I prevented her head from doing so. She was naturally in a state of shock and lucky to be alive but after a few minutes composed herself, then she and the family started to take stock of what other damage had been done. The television set was completely destroyed, a stone had been blown off the chimney stack and an impression of the chain holding a wash basin plug had been burnt into the porcelain of the basin. The lightning had scored a direct hit on Thorneys and at the same time had killed two cows in a field opposite that were sheltering under an Ash Tree which was also badly damaged. Thorneys had never been struck by lightning before despite its elevated position and we often wondered if it was a punishment for me falling out with the vicar!

About a month before the wedding, Jean and I had got the keys to Rose Cottage so we had moved quite a lot of items in. Jean had several items of furniture which belonged to her and we had been given several other items which were second hand and were no longer needed by their previous owners. We had bought a brand new bed and mattress, the Sleepeezee Beautyrest Connaught, which was an expensive five foot bed and in 1970 was unusual, as most people slept in beds six inches narrower. The only problem was that bedding for this wider bed was scarce and there was not as much choice of design or availability as there would have been with the then standard four foot six inch bed. Our wedding list had covered many household, kitchen and bathroom items so we had a good start when we settled into married life.

August 12th soon arrived but was rather a gloomy and threatening looking day. The wedding had been planned for twelve noon so I got changed into my suit and prepared for the drive to church. My mother when younger was not an emotional type but I could tell that she was trying to hold back the tears as she wished me the best of luck and I thanked her for everything that she had done for me up to now. I drove to Arkholme in my orange bomb and left it at Rose Cottage and walked the rest of the way to the church. I had arranged for it to be driven to Thorneys, I think by Peter, as I was not allowed anywhere near there in case I should catch sight of the bride. After the wedding Jean had wanted to leave the reception in the orange bomb as it was so different to anything else around at that time. In the evening we would return to Rose Cottage for our wedding night and start our honeymoon going off in Jean's car the following day, as it was much more reliable for the longer journey that we hoped to make. Very few English weddings then had an evening celebration to follow the reception, so after the reception was over, everyone would go home.

At the church my best man, Brian Hodgson, arrived, along with my groomsman, John Talbot. I had been best man at both of their weddings but as I had known Brian so much longer, he had to be my first choice. Jean's brother Peter was the other groomsman and he turned up shortly afterwards. I had expected to be very nervous but I wasn't and felt very comfortable and completely at ease greeting several of the guests as they arrived. At about ten to twelve Brian and I made our way into the church to sit in our appointed places, in preparation for the arrival of the Bride and her father. As is the custom they were slightly late but eventually the organ struck up and Jean accompanied by her father were walking towards me. I looked at Jean and could not believe how beautiful she looked and how very lucky I was to have her as my wife. As we made our vows to each other in the sight of God, I meant every word that I spoke and have always done my best to keep to those vows. When we were pronounced 'man and wife', I was the happiest person in the world. The actual ceremony was not taken by the Arkholme vicar but by a cousin of Jean's father called Noel Coleman who was really the Vicar of Silverdale. The Arkholme vicar was in attendance and supervised that the registers were correctly signed but we felt quite honoured that two clergymen had conducted our wedding. Outside the church afterwards everyone was in a happy mood congratulating us both as we tried to pose for the various photographers who were plentiful. I asked Jean if she had been nervous and told her that I wasn't in the least and she said that she had felt exactly the same with no nerves whatsoever.

We were driven back to Thorneys in the wedding car after confetti had been thrown and a handful stuffed down my back and arrived at the reception in a large marquee held on one of the lawns outside Thorneys. I was introduced to a large number of friends and Jean's relatives, many of whom I had never seen previously and could not remember them all, so hectic was the moment. There was a wonderful buffet which Jean's parents had ordered from a local caterer and bottles of bubbly flowed, seemingly never ending. We had none of it being so busy making sure that we spoke to every one of our guests and I did not drink any alcohol as I was driving afterwards. The time was getting close for us to leave and we both went upstairs in Thorneys to get changed. I think that I wore something comfortable and casual and Jean looked fantastic in a pink dress and matching hat. On the way out we passed Joan's husband Ramon, now my new brother-in-law, and he wished us a good time then burst out laughing and said 'Well you will have, won't you'! We also burst out laughing as his comments were not meant to be cheeky, it just came out that way but we all found it very funny. We eventually got away in the orange bomb nearly crashing into a car coming along the main road as I sped out of the entrance at Thorneys trying to avoid people attaching various objects to my car.

At last we were alone and married. I was driving along with my beautiful wife by my side and I was so very happy. Jean asked me if I had managed to eat anything at the reception and I told her that I had eaten nothing and was feeling hungry. Exactly the same thing had happened to her and she suggested that we look for somewhere to eat but not too close by in case any of our guests should spot us. We eventually decided to go to Sedbergh where we found a small restaurant and after ordering a meal spotted some customers of mine who recognised me. Fortunately I don't think they realised that I was newly married so after passing the time of day with them, we got on with eating our food before leaving and deciding what we should do next. We decided that we should try Kendal to see if we could kill some time there. When we were driving around we spotted a cinema so parked the car and decided to go to the pictures. The film showing was a new version of 'Goodbye Mr Chips' starring Petula Clark and Peter O'Toole. We got settled into the film and snuggled up together watching this very romantic and weepy story, which we both really enjoyed despite the film having got terrible ratings, as we found out later.

When we left the cinema it was getting dark and we made our way back to Rose Cottage, sneaking in to find a scene of devastation. Several of our guests had managed to open a window, climb in and open the front door, letting in several revellers. They had covered much of the house in confetti and made up an apple-pie bed. Jean was very upset and we both felt that our privacy had been seriously invaded. This really spoilt what had otherwise been an absolutely perfect day for us both and we cleared up things as best as possible. We had wanted an early night as we were setting off in the morning for our honeymoon and did not want to be too late getting away. The following morning we tidied up a little but eventually left some things until after we got back in order that we could get on the road. We had nothing specific planned and decided each day where we would go next and on this first day settled on Harrogate where we would find accommodation. We had saved a little money and had planned on being away for three or four nights depending on how our money held out but as we had been leaving Thorneys the previous day, Jean's father had pushed an envelope into the inside pocket of my jacket telling me to open it later, saying that it might come in useful. It certainly did as it contained sixty pounds, which meant that we could now have about a week away in good two and three star hotels.

On reaching Harrogate we did some shopping, grabbing a bite to eat, then went searching for somewhere to stay. We eventually settled on an impressive old-looking hotel called The Prospect and booked in. We were shown to a lovely first floor corner room with a window on each of two aspects and an en suite bathroom, quite uncommon then. We were delighted with the accommodation; I remember the room so well but cannot remember whether we had an evening meal in the hotel or ate out. The following day we were on the road and made our way to Lincolnshire, looking for a small town called Alford. There we found a suitable hotel right in the main town square and booked in for one night. It was only early in the afternoon so we went off exploring, firstly calling at the small village of Bilsby where my Great Grandfather and Great-Great Grandfather had both been vicars of the parish. We went to the vicarage, now a modern bungalow next to the church, and made contact with the vicar who gave us some useful information about one remaining elderly lady of ninety two years old who might remember my ancestors and where we might find her. We did indeed find her and she did remember my Great Grandfather but to my dismay related that in his old age had probably suffered from senile dementia and turned to drink after an otherwise unblemished career. Owing to his drunkenness he had been quietly pensioned off and forcibly retired. I quickly realised that delving too deep into family history can sometimes upset illusions that one might otherwise have had. After that we made our way to Mablethorpe, a lovely quaint seaside town, and then on to Cleethorpes before returning to our hotel to have an enjoyable evening meal together.

After breakfast the following morning we wanted to check out but could not find any staff in order to pay the bill. In the end I found the owners' accommodation, knocked on the door and was invited inside whilst I settled our account. In their flat was a beautiful parrot which was happily talking away and fascinated me. I asked why the parrot was not in the hotel bar where it was sure to be a great tourist attraction instead of hidden away in their flat. I was told that it had started off life in the hotel bar but the local customers had taught it a wide vocabulary of obscene language. It had become an embarrassing liability and had to be banished to their flat to prevent it from offending prospective customers and would now have to stay there indefinitely.

When we returned to the car we got out my road atlas and an old AA book and decided to go to Oundle in Northamptonshire to stay in a hotel called the Talbot. According to the AA book it served top quality food and this was going to be our one very special night where we would spend a little more than usual for slightly better accommodation than we were accustomed to. We rang in advance to book, to ensure that we did not have a wasted journey and when we arrived, drove into the courtyard of what seemed to be a very old coaching inn. The inside was very impressive and covered in old wood panels but despite its age was a very smart hotel, giving the impression of being steeped in history. We were shown to our room, walking along a corridor of squeaky wooden floorboards, and in our room was a beautiful feather bed. We had dinner there that evening, which was a superb Hungarian Goulash, and then retired to the amazing feather bed which was so comfortable.

Early the following day we set off for Somerset to a small hamlet called Curry Rivel. Jean wanted to stay in the village, having heard so much about it from her mother who had worked there for a family looking after their offspring as a children's nanny. After a longish journey taking us through Bath and stopping briefly at Wells to see the Cathedral, we eventually arrived but I remember nothing about where we stayed. Jean wanted to find the place where her mum had worked so long ago. The following morning, we eventually succeeded in finding the correct house called 'The Chestnuts', situated along a quiet road.

Neither of us had been to Cornwall before and decided that we should go, so off we went, driving through Devon, stopping at Exeter for lunch. We then continued into Cornwall, eventually finding a nice bed and breakfast establishment situated right underneath the television transmitter at Caradon Hill. After booking in and dropping off our suitcases we drove into Looe and Polperro, which were both very busy. In Polperro we went into an art shop selling paintings and both fell in love with a picture depicting a seascape painted by an artist called Prudence Turner. Jean has reminded me that the price was twenty five pounds, which we could afford but would use up all of our money, meaning that we would have to set off home the following morning. If we did not buy the painting, we could have another night's stay somewhere, prolonging our honeymoon. We pondered a long time and I could see that Jean really loved the painting as I did also. She eventually said that we should buy the painting to always remind us of how fantastic our honeymoon had been and that it would be a permanent reminder of that for the rest of our lives – this was better that one more night away. I agreed with her so we bought the painting and used up nearly all of our money, leaving us with just enough to pay for our bed and breakfast and the petrol to get us home. We had already bought enough food to have a picnic that afternoon, so we found a small secluded spot at Talland Bay nearby. This was a picturesque and deserted location so we sat looking out to sea, enjoying our food, watching the waves rolling in, enjoying these last moments of this wonderful time that would remain in our memories for ever.

We found that our accommodation was a busy spot as at breakfast time quite a lot of people were eating prior to heading off for the day.

We got away very early as we had a drive home which was in excess of three hundred miles, made easier by travelling along the new M5 motorway which had only been opened a few weeks beforehand. This meant that we improved on my estimate as to how long the journey would take. The drive back was very straightforward and we arrived in Arkholme during the early part of the afternoon, going straight to Thorneys first to tell the family that we were back. Everyone stopped work when we pulled into the drive and we were greeted like the proverbial prodigal children with hugs and kisses all round. After a cup of tea we wanted to get home to Rose Cottage to tidy up and unload our suitcases, return to reality and begin our married life in the normal way. We were both very tired and after having a light tea, we listened to the radio then had an early night.

The following morning a faint humming noise awoke me – it was noise of the milking machine from the farm across the road and although it was not really noisy, the sound was unfamiliar to my ears so had disturbed me. I looked at Jean still fast asleep beside me, she looked beautiful and I still could not believe how lucky I was to be married to her. Shortly afterwards she awoke and we got dressed and went downstairs for breakfast. We suddenly realised that we had a severe shortage of everyday crockery, which currently consisted of two medium sized bowls from the Dorset Pottery. These were fine for breakfast but they also had to be fine for dinner, tea and everything else as well and if there were two courses, we had to wash them before using them again to eat the next course. The local shop solved the problem where we bought some cheap plates, allowing us the luxury of having different plates for each course and the ability to now have dirty pots!

It was time to get down to reality and after the high of the wedding and honeymoon, we started to discuss what our plans and expectations would be for the future. Jean and I have always been able to talk to each other and be absolutely honest in what we say, even if it is sometimes not what we want to say or hear. That way we have always had total trust in each other through love, combined with openness and honesty. I asked Jean never to nag me as my mum had often done, as it was counterproductive and would have exactly the opposite effect as to what was intended. I also said that like any man I love the sight of a pretty girl and would always do so but if she promised not to be jealous, I promised that I would never ever touch anyone but her, as she had my undying love for life. That has always held true as she has never shown any jealousy whatsoever and I have never even thought about getting involved with anyone else. Shortly after we had first become engaged, Jean had made it very plain that she wanted children and I had endorsed her feelings as this was also an important part of marriage for me. We now got down to the question of when and Jean said that she would like our first child to be born before her thirtieth birthday. We also decided that the ideal family size for us would be four children if that was possible and in an ideal world, two boys then two girls, but the most important thing above all else was that everyone remained safe, well and healthy. This gave us about a year to settle down and get ourselves a little more financially secure before trying to start a family.

After the frenzy of our courtship and the busy time before our wedding, life settled down and suddenly we seemed less busy. After Jean finished work, she would wait for me to leave the shop so that we went home together every night except when the schools were on holiday, then I would use her car for work leaving her at Arkholme. Now that we were together we did not need two cars so I gave the orange bomb to Peter but a few weeks later, the floor dropped out and the car had to be scrapped, spending many years rotting away in a remote corner of a field at Thorneys until it was no more.

We soon got used to the routine of work and trying to get our home together, first of all buying a new bedroom carpet and then a new stairs carpet. We had already put down some rush matting in our tiny lounge and had built rocking chairs from kits and along with a room divider cum bookcase that had already belonged to Jean. We now had a cosy little refuge during wintertime, warmed by a coal fire with its back boiler to heat up the water. Our garden was almost two hundred feet long and nearly eighty feet wide at the widest point so on nice days when not working we spent a lot of time in the garden. For just over the first year of our married life we did not have a television set and after dark enjoyed what the radio had to offer.

For my birthday Jean bought a blue budgie in a cage for me, so we also now had a pet which gave us great pleasure. We also had a telephone installed, that being necessary for my work, as occasionally the police had to be able to contact me should there be any incident at the shop.

At Christmas we did not want to favour either side of our families so invited everyone to our house for Christmas dinner and they all came. We had a house full of people, a wonderful day and somehow managed to feed everyone on time with the help of both our mums who had become firm friends. I cannot remember exactly what happened at New Year but suspect that it was spent quietly with just the two of us and me performing the rituals taught to me by my father, to let the New Year in and the Old Year out, putting a piece of coal on the fire on the way through the house, in true Geordie fashion.

Reg at back of 9 Ffrances Passage c1963

Reg with his first car outside 45 Portland Street, Lancaster c1967.
Younger brother Fred is the child on the right hand side.

Reg and Jean, 1969 at Eyemouth on their first holiday together

Reg and Jean's wedding day, 12th August 1970

1971

We had now settled down to married life and the routine that went with it, up in the morning, driving to work together and back home again at the end of the day. We kept on buying bits and pieces for the house as and when we could afford them and were saving up to have a holiday towards the end of the year. We decided to change Jean's Mini car for a minivan as we thought that it would be more practical for when we would have children. During springtime we hunted around the dealers until we found one that had a minivan in stock. We already had a buyer for Jean's car, a friend of Peter's who had just passed his driving test and was looking for a reliable vehicle. As a minivan was considerably cheaper than a car, the money from the car sale paid for a brand new Mini Van which we found much more useful for carrying large items.

We occasionally were meeting up with friends for the odd evening out but as many of them were now married or about to get married, out social life had quietened down quite considerably. When the winter was over and the weather had warmed up, we spent a lot of time in the garden, cutting grass, tidying up and getting ready to start planting vegetables. In the first year we only planted potatoes as we still had a lot more ground to clear but the crop was very successful, which spurred us on to do even better in the future. Periodically we got invited out to tea with one or the other of our parents and often they would also come to us.

During the summer I got home one evening and pulled up in Rose Cottage drive in the van. I cannot remember why Jean had not been working but when I arrived back she was outside gardening and looked fantastic in a short white top and slightly dishevelled because of the effort of hard work. I suggested that this might be a good time to start our family and she agreed. Not long afterwards she confirmed that she was pregnant and our first child was due the following March; we could not believe our luck in conceiving at the first attempt. When we broke the news to everyone after twelve weeks, they were all delighted and looking forward to future events. All was not initially well, however, as Jean started being very sick, not just in the mornings but sometimes for days on end, but eventually things did improve.

We had been invited to go and stay in Stocksfield, Northumberland by an ex working colleague of Jean's called Nellie. She had married her husband Colin Shrimpton shortly after Jean and I were married and they had moved to be close to Colin's work, teaching history at one of the colleges in Newcastle-on-Tyne. Nellie was always great fun, a very entertaining person, fantastic mimic and the only lady that I know who can use obscene language and still sound like a lady. We had three fantastic days staying with them and discovered whilst we were there that she was also pregnant, expecting her baby at about the same time as ours.

About this time Jean's brother Peter went off to Newcastle University to study electrical engineering and soon settled living in the Jesmond Dene area. This was great as it gave us an excuse to visit the north east even more although Peter often did come home at weekends bringing new friends with him.

My mum and dad were suddenly facing a crisis as my dad had been made redundant from his workplace. About the time that I was born my dad was demobilised from the Royal Air Force and had worked for two or three years as a cellulose sprayer for a nearby garage. He had then become a bus driver for Lancaster City Transport and in the late 1950s worked for Nelsons, a factory on Caton Road, Lancaster. Amongst other things Nelsons manufactured a synthetic yarn which my dad inspected before it was sent out to customers. He trudged the streets and made lots of enquiries and within five days he had found a job at Top Rank Services on the motorway filling cars and lorries with fuel. This suited him perfectly as he loved cars and this was the perfect environment for him.

My mum, however, still had a wage coming in as she was still working for the school meals service. She had left work for a few years when my brother Fred was born but after Fred had started school she began working at the Lancaster Boys' Grammar School and had later moved on to the Lancaster Girls' Grammar School.

Our friends David and Carol were due to get married in October and I offered to take their wedding pictures – a foolish mistake as the weather was dull and I felt that I had not done it the justice that it deserved. The day nevertheless was a happy one and it was great to see two wonderful friends of ours tying the knot.

We had booked to go on holiday during Jean's October break from school and had decided to tour Germany in our Mini Van. We caught the overnight ferry from Hull, arriving in Rotterdam the following morning and from there drove through Holland into Germany until we reached a small town called Bruchsal just beyond Cologne. We stayed in a small hotel called the 'Kaiserhof' where we booked in for one night including evening meal and breakfast. The evening meal came as a banquet on a silver platter and would have fed a family of six people, so we did our best, but despite being stuffed to a point where we could hardly walk, we made little impression on the quantity of food provided. The following morning we had a small breakfast and then drove south towards Koblentz and on to a small town called Oberwesel where we stayed the next night at a hotel called the 'Goldener Pfropfenzieher' or translated, 'The Golden Corkscrew'. This was a lovely hotel within sight of the Rhein where we had a luxuriously comfortable bed and a more modest meal this time, with a bottle of local wine before retiring for the night. The following morning we spent a little time exploring the town and surrounding area and fell in love with this little place. Before leaving we purchased some bread, wurst and sauerkraut, which allowed us to make sandwiches for the next couple of days to get us through lunchtimes.

We carried on further south to Mannheim where we spent the next night. We had been recommended a hotel there but when we arrived it was all closed up for the winter season but fortunately we did find somewhere else to stay. The following day we carried on further south but on reaching Heidelberg it occurred to us that if we did not start off back, we would never get the Saturday evening return ferry from Rotterdam and it was now Thursday morning. We immediately did an about turn and headed north until reaching a small town called Laasphe in the mid-afternoon. We found a small hotel in a quiet street which had vacancies and stayed there during Thursday night. We had an intimate evening meal in the hotel as we were the only people dining and on Friday morning continued further north. On reaching the outskirts of Dortmund we got stuck in one of the largest traffic jams that we have ever experienced. We never moved for ninety minutes but used the time productively to make sandwiches and eat a picnic lunch so when the traffic did get moving again we were duly refreshed.

We eventually ended up in Emmerich, a small town close to the Dutch border, which meant that we could get to the ferry with ease the following day. Our hotel in Emmerich did not serve evening meals so we found a small restaurant in the town and had a meal there. After breakfast the following morning we crossed the Dutch border and headed west until we reached Rotterdam. In 1971 there was no by-pass so I was dreading trying to find my way through the town centre to access the correct road out to Europoort where we were to catch the ferry. When we reached Rotterdam there were no signs at all but on reaching the middle of the town, I spotted a road heading west which my instincts told me was roughly in the right direction so I took that road. A mile or two down the road we saw signs, which to our relief told us that we were heading in the right direction. We arrived at the docks just after midday so knew that we were in for a long wait as the ship did not sail until six thirty. There was, however, a superb cafeteria so we sat in there for about three hours having a meal and then drinking coffee until at last going outside when it was nearer the time for boarding.

We had a meal on board the ship then went back to our cabin for a good night's sleep before arriving back in Hull on the Sunday morning. Fortunately Jean had been really well on our trip meaning that we both had a happy and memorable holiday and had really enjoyed our first holiday abroad together.

The drive home from Hull was very straightforward until we reached Gargrave where we needed the toilets which were down a quiet side road. After using the toilets we set off again in the van back down this quiet road when Jean started screaming at me. It then occurred to me that I had got so used to continental driving, I was driving down the wrong side of the road and had anything been coming in the opposite direction, disaster would have struck. Ever since that day I have always been most vigilant on returning home; I now always consciously think before getting in the car in case the same were to happen again. We arrived home to be greeted by happy and relieved families that we were still intact and Jean was keeping well. Sadly that situation was not to last and Jean started to feel ill again shortly afterwards and had to visit her doctor and a specialist doctor in Morecambe on an alternate weekly basis.

I don't remember much about Christmas or New Year as I was so pre-occupied with Jean's state of health.

1972

J ean continued to feel unwell and was getting regular medical supervision from doctors and pre-natal hospital visits. She was advised to finish work immediately and rest to see if that improved matters as her ankles were swelling and she was still constantly feeling unwell. Early in March I had visited the hospital with her when a nurse took me aside saying that they were very concerned that no heartbeat from the baby could be found and that we might lose it but under no circumstances to tell Jean. When we got home, I immediately told her what had been said to me as I has always promised that there would never be secrets between us. This at least prepared us for the tragedy that came on 16th March when Jean gave birth to our stillborn daughter in the Queen Victoria Hospital, Morecambe. I cannot write any further on this subject as the pain is still too great and although it is a situation with which we have both learned to live, it is the greatest sorrow that has ever befallen us.

When Jean came home I managed to get a few days off work and we spent some time consoling each other and trying to get our lives back on track. During that time we saw very few people and received few visitors. I am sure that friends did not know what to say and felt awkward, and in their situation I think that I would have felt the same, so most of them stayed away. One day in Lancaster I was shopping when a grocery shop manager who I knew took me aside and quietly said that he was so sorry to hear what had happened and that he and his wife had experienced an identical mishap. He knew exactly how we were feeling and said that other children would come along and things would get better. I was very much cheered up by that and even more so when one evening Dave and Carol Silver turned up at Arkholme having just heard what had happened. They had no car and at that time there was no bus service but they had scrounged a one-way lift with a friend who was going to Kirkby Lonsdale and had no idea how they would get back to Lancaster but gave no thought to that, such was their concern for us. We were delighted to see them and their visit dragged us out of our self-pity, being so moved by their gesture of concern and true friendship. That moment was the turning point for us to look ahead to the future and start again. I was more than happy to drive them back to Lancaster afterwards with Carol in the passenger seat and Dave bundled into the back of the van. Just after I got back to work, I bumped into Judith in Lancaster Town Centre and she looked terrible. It turned out that she had been pregnant at the same time as Jean, gone full term and also had a stillbirth. I could not believe this horrible coincidence but knew only too well what she was suffering and felt so very sorry for her, as she did for us.

Next time Jean saw the doctor she asked him when it was advisable to start again trying for a family and he said that after the six weeks postnatal period, we could start as soon as we wished. We tried immediately again as soon as was possible and to our astonishment Jean became pregnant immediately. This time she had constant medical supervision throughout but after a small bout of morning sickness she was fine and kept in really good health. We managed a few days' holiday in Whitley Bay staying with relatives but took it easy and did not tear around as we had done in the past.

With Jean being at home all of the time now we at last purchased a television set and moved into the modern age, despite it being black and white as very few colour sets were around then. When I was at work she spent much of the time pottering around in the garden and growing vegetables which had now extended to peas and beans as well as potatoes.

At the shop Keith Duffy had now become a most useful and very experienced assistant so we were constantly busy with the business doing really well. Customers had now got used to the shop without Mr Robertson and had confidence in the way that we dealt with them and our sales figures continued to rise. Mrs Robertson was quite a frequent visitor and by now I would often drop her off at Hest Bank before driving home. We were becoming quite close and if she asked, I would help her with paying bills and keeping her finances straight. In the early days I think that she had been a little jealous about my love for Jean but now she had accepted it and also loved Jean. She had now really become the granny that I had lost so long ago and I used to enjoy helping her as I had come to love her as a family member.

During this period Mrs Robertson had to go into hospital for a routine procedure but getting out was not quite as straightforward, as the doctors did not want her to go home immediately without supervision. She asked me if I would go and stay for a few days but this was not possible. After conferring with Jean we offered to have her at Rose Cottage for a week after which time it was considered she could manage at home on her own. As I was at work during most days, it fell on Jean to look after her but she was in fact no trouble and they got on really well together and became very close. After a week she went back home and managed perfectly well but she had now become so much part of our family, ever afterwards she was always included in most of our family events that took place.

Jean continued to be closely monitored by her doctor backed up by the hospital. Every Monday, I had to take in a large bottle containing her urine sample for twenty four hours up to midnight Sunday. Without going into graphic detail I can only say that filling it proved a challenge for her and without my assistance in helping her to aim accurately into a large funnel, she would not have managed. This did, however, cause much hilarity between us and it is experiences like this that make the bond between a couple so much stronger. The sample was required to monitor her oestrogen levels and give an early warning should anything start to go wrong; this time, however, everything was going very right.

At the beginning of December my brother-in-law Ramon had suddenly been taken ill at work and rushed into hospital by ambulance. No one knew what was wrong but the following day he was diagnosed as having had a brain haemorrhage. When told, I was so shocked that I rushed to the toilet thinking that I was going to be sick, realising that he probably would not live. At that moment in time I don't think that most of the family understood the seriousness of his condition but this is what had killed my cousin George and I knew that Ramon's chances were slim. I conveyed my feelings to Jean who was shocked to hear of my pessimism and had not realised that the situation was so serious. Three days later he died, he was only twenty nine years old and left Jean's sister Joan a widow and his young seven year old son Tony without a father. This was an absolute tragedy, we had all loved Ramon so much with his easy going, laid back manner and his funeral was a very difficult affair for the whole family.

Christmas and New Year are a blur and I cannot remember what happened at all but Ramon's death put a dampener on all celebrations, so festivities this year were somewhat muted.

1973

F ortunately Jean was still keeping really well and showing none of the signs that had blighted us during this period last year; time was going by quickly and we were soon into the beginning of March. Our baby was now a little overdue so it was arranged that Jean would go into the Royal Lancaster Infirmary on March 8th to be induced the following day. That turned out to be unnecessary as she started in labour during the morning without intervention. I called in to see her in the early afternoon and said that I wished to be present at the birth as it had only very recently been a possibility for the father to be involved. I was told that Jean would not deliver for an hour or two so to come back about forty five minutes later. I said that I would wait outside the door and reiterated that I wanted to be present should things move on. About thirty minutes later, I was told to come in as our baby was now very imminent and not long afterwards our son 'Andrew Lyndon' was born. We were ecstatic and joyful at the sight of our new baby and for me, it was the first time of witnessing a birth. I was so appreciative of what my wife had to go through to achieve this, my love and respect for her was even stronger than it had been before. I was so glad that I had not listened to the medical staff as had I done so, I would have missed this wonderful event. I am still sure to this day that they had deliberately tried to get rid of me, as at that time they had still not come to terms with, or really wanted fathers being present whilst their wives were in labour.

A few days later I arrived at the hospital to take Jean and Andrew (Andy) home in our minivan which was now perfect for popping a carry cot into. No health and safety in those days, with the carry cot just sat in the back of the van, although I did drive extra slowly and very safely with our precious cargo. On returning to Rose Cottage we quickly got Andy into the house and settled down; we then looked at each other as mutual panic set in. 'What do we do now?' we said in unison and Jean said, 'What have we done?' as we both looked at this helpless baby who depended on us for everything. To say that we were in total confusion was the understatement of the year and at about eight thirty in the evening we realised that we had forgotten to have our tea!

The next day was not a lot better. Jean was upstairs in the bathroom seeing to Andy and I was downstairs washing pots when there was a knock on the door. I turned off the tap, answered the door and let in Jean's elderly doctor who had called to check that she and Andy were ok. After he had spoken with Jean and then with me, he left but only after we had a row with him, after refusing a smallpox vaccination for Andy. After he left Jean enquired why she could hear a trickling sound in the kitchen and when I got there, found the floor covered in water which was about to encroach out of the doorway. When the doctor called, I had turned off the tap and the flow of water had stopped but I had not turned it fully so when Jean turned off the upstairs tap to come down for the doctor, the downstairs tap had started flowing and flooded everything whilst we were speaking to him. The drawers under the sink were full of water and the pans and crockery in the cupboards underneath had also filled up. Jean and

Andy went upstairs again whilst I mopped up, laid newspapers down the hallway to the front door and proceeded to put all of the wet items on the newspapers. Just as I had finished doing that, there was another knock on the front door; this time it was the health visitor who looked perplexed at the trail of soggy newspapers covered in pots, pans and crockery all the way from the front door to a wet kitchen floor covered in upended drawers drying out. I gave her a sickly grin and assured her that we really did have everything under control, although it did not appear that way, and that our present situation was a temporary domestic emergency which would be quickly resolved. She did not look very convinced but after talking to Jean and checking Andy, she left, still looking very uncomfortable about our competency in the skills of parenthood.

From that moment things could only get better and they did as we settled into the routine of looking after a baby and got used to the idea of having this new person in our lives. One nice day we decided to take Andy for his first outing, putting him in his pram and setting off to walk down towards the church. On the way we met one or two neighbours who all wished us well, each of them giving Andy a small monetary gift. On reaching the church we met the vicar who congratulated us on Andy's birth, then asked Jean if she would like to be churched. I had vaguely heard of this custom in the Church of England but thought that it had died out in medieval times. The vicar assured us that this was not the case and although many women chose not to bother, it was a form of thanksgiving for the wellbeing of the mother after the dangers of childbirth. We could not argue against that and said that Jean would like to be churched but when would it be appropriate to do it? 'Right now' was his answer and before we knew it we were in church with this short ritual of only about five minutes taking place. When it was over the vicar informed us that there was not a statutory charge for this service but it was customary to give a donation; no wonder he wanted to do it there and then! The problem was that we had hadn't left the house equipped with money, not having anticipated this unexpected expense, but then suddenly realised that we had Andy's money given to us by kind neighbours. We had a quick count up and gave that money to the vicar then had to reimburse Andy's gift money when we got home. Oh, the shame of it, the very first time we had ever taken our son out, he had to lend money to his parents to get them through the day!

When home for the weekend, my brother-in-law Peter often popped in with various new friends that he had made at university and called one Sunday with a very quiet and shy young man who hardly spoke a word to us. It turned out that he hardly spoke to Jean's parents either, despite staying with them and they thought him most strange. The young man was called Rowan Atkinson who despite this shyness has done rather well for himself since and still remains a friend of Peter.

Our social lives were now put completely on hold as we concentrated on the responsibilities of family life and with the exception of a few local events, we spent a lot of time at home, gardening and growing vegetables. Every other Saturday I brought Jean and Andy to Lancaster and whilst I was at work, my parents would look after Andy whilst Jean went shopping and when she had finished would wait for me to finish work. The alternate Saturdays when she and Andy were not in Lancaster they spent at Thorneys with her parents. This gave both sides of our respective families regular contact with Andy and him the chance to get used to all of his grandparents.

We were so wrapped up getting used to our new family life, we did not get involved with all that was happening in Lancaster. My sister Marilyn had met Bill Lupton and wedding preparations were now well underway. Bill was a quiet chap and several years older than Marilyn but they seemed very happy and we were happy for them.

The wedding took place on a beautiful summer day and the

reception was in the room above the Alexandra Hotel on the corner of King Street and Thurnham Street, Lancaster. All was well until the early evening when my dad suddenly disappeared. It turned out that he had fallen and felt shaken up and unwell, so had gone home. I was very worried and went after him but he assured me that he would be alright and persuaded me to go back to the wedding reception.

Marilyn and Bill went off to the Isle of Man for their honeymoon but the honeymooning was short-lived because soon after they arrived there was a disaster. A large leisure complex called Summerlands suffered a horrendous fire with many lives lost and lots of others injured. The Manx Government appealed to any holidaymakers medically qualified to volunteer and help at the hospital. Marilyn was now a qualified nurse so she spent most of her honeymoon working at the hospital attending to the dead and injured. Eventually they returned and said that they had been in Summerlands but had left only moments before the fire had started otherwise the outcome could have been very different.

During the August Bank Holidays we had a few days' holiday in Seahouses staying again with Ann and Bart who were getting to know us quite well by now and they were more than happy to have Andy despite the disruption of night time feeds. The weather was excellent and during the days we went off exploring the delights of Northumberland and in the evenings Ann and Bart insisted that we go out whilst they did babysitting duties. Although the holiday was short, we had a wonderful time and were quite sorry when it came to an end and had to return home.

We had always made it known that when we had our own family, we would spend Christmas at home but everyone was welcome to join us. I cannot remember what actually happened but think that during the period between Christmas and New Year most of our family members paid us a visit.

1974

We were now firmly entrenched with family life and a routine soon set in. As before, Jean was visiting Lancaster on alternate Saturdays and the business was doing well.

Five years had passed since I had been made a partner in the business and I did at last make my final payment for the one eighth of the partnership. Customers had now at last got used to me and our turnover and profits had risen considerably. It then suddenly occurred to me that with the value of the business rising so much, buying the rest of the business from Mrs Robertson was soon going to be impossible and I was slowly working myself out of a job. I put the situation to Mrs Robertson who at first was very unhappy that I should buy her out but when she realised that it would take another five years to do so giving her an increased and regular income during that time she agreed. She was still worried, however, that it would diminish her status and that our friendship might come to an end as now she depended on me for so much help and advice. I promised her that nothing would change and that I would always help her in any way I could and kept that promise until the end of her life.

I was now sole proprietor in the business but having to pay Mrs

Robertson meant that for the next two or three years in particular, Jean and I were extremely hard up. Jean had always wanted to have our first two children close together so by springtime, Jean was pregnant again. The pregnancy went really well and Jean was enjoying such good health that she was able to do light gardening and we all had three days in Seahouses during the late summer staying again with Ann and Bart. On the return journey home we stopped off at Cullercoats where I had an appointment at the coastguard station to take a Morse test.

For several years I had been interested in amateur radio and had recently passed my City and Guilds Examination 365 to enable me to hold a transmitting licence. I needed to pass the Morse test to enable me to apply for a full licence and in those days it was possible to take the test at most coastguard stations. I was overjoyed when the coastguard said that I had passed, which enabled me to hold a full licence, and on returning home applied to the Home Office for it. A few days later I was given my call sign of G4DLP which enabled me to contact other radio amateurs anywhere in the world and it is a hobby that I still enjoy right up to the present day.

On November 19th Jean started in labour during the morning and as I was at work in Lancaster, her dad said that he would drive her to the Royal Lancaster Infirmary. Winter had started early and the roads were very icy that morning and they had only got about three miles down the road when Jean's dad lost control of his car. He skidded all of the way down a hill and ended up in the car park of The Redwell Inn just outside Arkholme and although they were both shaken, they and the car were undamaged so they carried on, albeit a little more slowly. In the early afternoon, I got a phone call to tell me that Jean was in the labour ward and hurried from the shop to be with her. I arrived at the labour ward to a situation of controlled chaos as four women who had been induced that morning had all gone into labour at the same time and Jean was the last of four women who had arrived at the hospital as their childbirths were imminent. With eight women all giving birth at about the same time, the labour ward was full and Jean had been put into a side room.

A midwife asked me whether or not I had ever seen a birth before and when I told her that I had, she put a red buzzer switch in my hand and told me to press the switch should I see any sign of the head appearing. She did, however, keep popping back every two or three minutes and was there at the crucial moment when she was needed. I assisted as best as possible but the birth was very straightforward and Jean was soon handed our new baby boy. We hadn't finally agreed on what to call him but as she held him in her arms she said to me, 'I want to call him Matthew'. How could I disagree? After all that she had been through.

I had to leave after that but went back to hospital for evening visiting to be greeted with the news that Matthew was in an incubator as the paediatrician had detected a heart murmur. Jean seemed quite calm but I was almost sick with worry; the staff had explained to Jean that this was not uncommon as the organs of many newborn babies had not completely developed but at this moment I was unconvinced. When I visited the following day, Matthew was out of the incubator which gave me greater reassurance. After a week Andrew and I went to collect Jean and Matthew but Jean was most upset when she saw Andrew, as her mum had cut his hair and he looked quite grown up, not her baby boy that she had left behind just a week ago.

When we had taken Andrew home we had tucked him into his carry cot with lots of bedding to keep him warm but he had turned bright red and was sweating and clearly too warm so we had to remove some of the covers. We discovered that Matthew was just the opposite and needed plenty of covers as he seemed to feel the cold much more than Andrew. We were now experienced parents and all of the panic and problems of last time were in the past. We had our tea on time and enjoyed a little leisure time in the evening whilst both of our boys were sleeping.

Christmas was wonderful with Andrew enjoying his presents and although Matthew was too young to appreciate the occasion, it was wonderful to be at home with our two young boys. About this time the Rev Cairns had once again suggested that Jean be churched so it was done and this time we went prepared with some money!

1975

E arly during the year Arkhome village school was threatened with closure and there was a public meeting to discuss this. I contacted a friend of mine called Graham Curwen who worked in the education office directly under the chief education officer. Graham had been brought up in the village of Pilling and was very sympathetic to each village having its own school wherever possible. Graham also explained to me that his boss had made a huge error of judgement in authorising an expensive improvement scheme for the school in Whittington just three miles away when the school had just four pupils and little chance of the numbers increasing in the foreseeable future. Arkholme had about forty five pupils with a projected increase to about sixty within five years. The chief education officer was trying to justify his position by claiming that the improved school building at Whittington was more suitable than Arkholme School and it would be better to bus all of the Arkholme children to Whittington rather than four Whittington children to Arkholme. Melling across the river was theoretically to be involved in this scheme but, like Arkholme, it was a church school and the vicar there had a reputation for being a formidable opponent so the chief education officer decided not to interfere with him.

In the greatest confidence I passed all of this information to my father-in-law who was an Arkholme School governor so at subsequent meetings he was able to ask awkward, searching and embarrassing questions. Graham kept me informed and told me that his boss was furious that the Arkholme School governors seemed so well informed as he had expected the closure to be a pushover but knew that he was now losing the battle. At what was going to be the deciding meeting in Hornby, the Akrholme Vicar, Rev Norman Cairns, stood up to defend the position of Arkholme School, completely lost his temper with the chief education officer and in full flow with his heated speech, collapsed and died of a heart attack. The chief education officer threw in the towel, closed Whittington School and Arkholme School was saved. The chief education officer left Lancaster shortly afterwards but I cannot remember whether he took up another position or retired. My friend Graham Curwen was so fed up with the education situation that he decided to make a sideways move into administration in the NHS Primary Trust of which he eventually became chief in the Lancaster area. For his work there and with various other organisations he was awarded a well-deserved MBE in 2013.

This put us into a personal quandary as we had arranged with the Arkholme Vicar, Rev Cairns, to have Matthew baptised but the vicar had died just five days before the baptism was due to take place. We waited for a day or two but heard nothing from anyone so cancelled the celebrations that we had arranged for after the baptism. On the day before it was due to take place we were contacted by The Rev Booth, Vicar of Whittington, who had been reading the Arkholme Church appointments book and told us that he would do the baptism. We had to tell him that we had cancelled all arrangements, as until he contacted us we did not know what was happening. He was a delightful, gentle, old fashioned vicar and sounded quite crestfallen but was very helpful in organising another date a few weeks later.

Matthew was called back to the hospital to have his heart checked and we duly arrived for the appointment. He had been fed before leaving home but we had to drive to Lancaster first and because parking at the hospital was difficult, we had left the van at my parents and taken Matthew to the hospital in his pram. We waited for what seemed like an eternity and eventually saw the consultant, albeit over an hour late. By now Matthew was hungry, howling the place down and would not be pacified. The consultant could not hear Matthew's heart because of the noise, so the consultation was curtailed and reorganised for a later date, when thankfully everything was alright.

During the summer Arkholme got its new vicar, a man called George Worthington. George was probably in his late thirties and a family man with his wife Margaret and three young children. He was a delightful and enthusiastic man and was quickly embraced by most of the villagers who were soon filling his church. He got involved with every village activity that he could and his energy seemed boundless. One day he asked me why I had never been confirmed in the Church of England. I explained that I had come from a Presbyterian background and after falling out with his predecessor before I was married, I had not felt inclined to become one of the flock. George asked me if I still felt that way and I said that under him I would like to be confirmed as I was now enjoying church activities. I told him that since being a boy I had a strong Christian belief and felt now felt ready to commit to the Church of England although I would always have strong ecumenical feelings. Shortly after being confirmed I became a sidesman at the church, which pleased my father-in-law who was a church warden and on the parochial church council. By now Jean was also on the parochial church council so we became heavily involved with church activities.

Once again we spent three days in Seahouses with Ann and Bart. Andy was getting used to them by now and Matthew took to them also. As before, they told us to go out in the evenings whilst they babysat which by now they quite enjoyed. Their two boys, Graeme and Craig, were a lot older than our boys, so it was a quite a novelty for them to have a baby and toddler around.

Christmas was wonderful: Andrew was nearing three years old and Matthew had just turned one and we had a lovely day doing all of the Christmas things and playing with the boys. On Boxing Day Evening at 7.00pm members of the Parochial Church Council and their spouses were invited to the vicarage for Christmas refreshments. We thanked George Worthington for the invitation but explained that we could not leave the boys and as Jean's parents would be going so there would be no babysitters. George said that he expected the event to finish about 8.30pm and if Jean's mum and dad were prepared to leave about twenty minutes early to babysit, we could pop along for the final few minutes. This seemed to be an ideal arrangement which suited everyone, so Jean and I arrived at the vicarage at about 8.15pm. Everyone there were finishing off cups of tea, coffee, mince pies and Christmas cake and the atmosphere was very jovial but although quickly seated we were not offered anything. After a few minutes we were feeling rather awkward having had not been offered anything and all the other guests were leaving. We stood up but George told us to sit down as he showed everyone else out and bid them good night and final season's greetings. George returned with a big grin on his face, looked at me and said, 'Shall we get out the beers?' opening a cupboard door revealing a considerable amount of alcohol. He explained that most of the Parochial Church Council being elderly and traditional probably would not have approved but now only we remained he thought that we would like a proper drink and that he was ready for one as well. We really enjoyed the evening and stayed talking to him and Margaret and comparing notes about our children.

New Year at the moment was a quiet affair and we often went to bed early in case we were disturbed during the night.

1976

This was a year of family weddings as far as I remember. Early in the year Jean's sister Joan married Dick Haston, a divorced farmer who was a close neighbour to Jean's parents, so after the wedding Joan and her son Tony moved to Lane End Farm, Arkholme.

The shop continued to thrive and I was kept very busy at work as well as at home. We were growing and freezing lots of vegetables, as well as storing our own potatoes. I had started beekeeping with my two homemade hives being sited at 'Thorneys', Jean's parents' house. By now we had acquired twelve hens so were completely self-sufficient in eggs with a surplus that we used to sell to friends, which paid for their feed. We had also acquired a goat called 'Gretchen', which had originally lived on the Ripley School Farm in Lancaster, being looked after by my brother Fred who was now fourteen years old. The teacher who was in charge of both Fred and the goat was a man called Bob Young and he was leaving, so the goat had to go. One evening we got a hurried phone call from Fred and within an hour my dad arrived in his car with both Fred and the goat.

We knew absolutely nothing about goats and Gretchen was in milk so had to be milked twice a day. Overnight we shut her up in our outside loo so that she had some shelter and the next day let her loose in the garden. A few hours later we were horrified to find that she had stripped the bark off most of our apple trees and that she was a four legged vandal. We very quickly purchased a tether so that we could control her movements and we now became self-sufficient in milk and quickly learned about goatkeeping.

My dad had just changed his job again as Top Rank Motorway Services had a new management team which insisted that anyone over sixty five must retire. My dad was sixty seven but still wanted to work, so immediately contacted Loxhams Garage on Thurnham Street, Lancaster and they gave him a similar job there and then. They had contacted him previously and told him there was a job waiting for him if he ever needed it and when the time came, they kept their word.

I was still drawing very little wages from the shop in order that I could pay Mrs Robertson and when my accountant saw how little money we were living on he thought that I was cooking the books. Nothing could have been further from the truth and I explained that we were living the good life, being practically self-sufficient in milk, eggs, peas, beans, lettuce, potatoes and honey. We had apples, pears and damsons from our trees and picked a lot of fruit such as blackberries from the hedgerows. At the end of the season Jean's dad always had a glut of tomatoes when clearing out his greenhouses, so gave them to us. We froze everything freezable such as tomato puree, apple puree, peas, beans and soft fruit. We used to get one pint of green top milk a day from the farm, poured off the cream each day and saved it in the fridge. The remainder of the milk we used and when there was sufficient cream used to shake it continuously in a large sweet jar to make our own butter. We purchased two large sackfuls of wheat from a local farmer and used to grind it into flour in a coffee grinder, then Jean baked it into wholemeal bread. We still did not have a washing machine and Jean did much of the washing outside the back door in a dolly tub using a posser. With a young family we had virtually no social life so never spent any money in pubs, restaurants or cinemas etc. When I was not at work, I was so busy at home helping Jean with the boys and all of our food production I had no spare time anyway. When my accountant did all of the sums he said that everything made sense but insisted that I should give myself a thirty three percent wage increase just to make everything a little more credible.

We could not afford alcohol so used to make our own wine with some of the fruit that we had grown or foraged for. There was frequently a plastic bucket of fermenting alcohol in our bathroom airing cupboard, the first stage before clearing and bottling it. One evening we kept hearing noises upstairs and eventually realised that the boys were out of bed and in the bathroom. We rushed upstairs to find that they had opened the airing cupboard door and were scooping cupped handfuls of the fermenting liquid into their mouths. Their pyjamas and hands were stained bright red and they had to be cleaned up and given a fresh set of pyjamas before being severely scolded and put back to bed. I don't know how much they had drunk but they certainly slept well that night. The wine sadly had to be thrown away as we did not know where their hands had been before being inserted into the bucket, so we lost our six bottle production on that occasion.

Jean's sister Joan had become pregnant and was due to give birth in February the following year.

My brother-in-law Peter was still at Newcastle University and had now got his degree in electrical engineering but was staying on to get his doctorate. He had been joined by Ruth Crossley, his girlfriend since their schooldays, who was studying to become a medical doctor. They had decided to get married, which meant that they could pool their resources, making accommodation cheaper. During the late summer they were married at Burton-in-Kendall so they returned to University as a married couple.

In late Autumn we decided that our faithful minivan was getting a little cramped. We had got the garage to mount two old car seats in the back to which were fastened child seats but the boys were growing so we decided to have a new car. We decided on a Datsun Sunny blue estate car which we purchased from the dealers in Kendal. This was sheer luxury as it had an efficient heater and a good radio. It turned out to be very reliable and we were delighted with it. It happened to be the very first Japanese car in Arkholme and at first our friends and neighbours were very dubious about it. They speculated that if it went wrong, repairs could be difficult and we should have bought a British car. I pointed out to them that both my father-in-law and my sister had recently purchased British cars which were both currently off the road. My father in law's car had been damaged by the post van whilst parked outside the school and my sister's car had been damaged following a blow out from the front nearside tyre. After eight weeks they were still off the road, as all of the British car workers were on strike and spares were impossible to obtain. I also pointed out to them that the Japanese do not strike and if I suffered any misfortune, I would probably have my car back on the road in well under eight weeks. That did the trick and no one gave me any more grief about my car.

When Christmas came, George Worthington gathered together a large band of carol singers of which I was one and we had a jolly evening going round the village singing for many households and raising funds for the church. I think that several of us finished up at the Bay Horse Pub, a rare treat for me in those days. I don't remember George inviting the Parochial Church Council round to his house again and think that he had done it previously to get better acquainted with everyone.

1977

On 18th February Jean's sister Joan gave birth to her daughter Suzie, giving Tony a little sister.

We continued to be very busy at home and the shop was going from strength to strength. Jean had become pregnant again but right from the beginning had felt unwell. We decided not to tell anyone until she had reached twelve weeks but just before that time she started to miscarry. I rang the doctor immediately but before anything could be done events overtook us. She had to rest for a short while but soon we thought things were getting back to normal. She was still spending alternate Saturdays in Lancaster and on the next one after this event realised that all was not well and my parents had to call for an emergency ambulance which rushed her into hospital for a D and C operation. After a few days she was a lot better and things at last slowly got back to normal.

A new family moved into Arkholme, into the old station building which had been partially modernised. They were called Jim and Phyllis Whittaker with their two children Susan and Peter. Susan was about the same age as Andrew and Peter the same age as Matthew. Jim was quite well known, however, as he had periodically appeared on television in his part time job as a comedian under his stage name Jim Bowen, his full time job being a teacher. He appeared at our house one day to invite the boys to a birthday party for Peter, joined in many village events and soon became a familiar face around the village and eventually the whole country when he became nationally famous with his 'Bullseye' quiz show four years later.

For many years I had not had any contact with my cousin Kath or her daughter Sue but had visited her in Berwick-on-Tweed when we were last in Seahouses and as a result, Sue, now a young woman of twenty years old, came to stay with us for a few days. Whilst she was with us she amused the boys who soon got used to her and thought the world of her.

By summer Jean was pregnant again, being very careful and keeping quite well. As before, we decided to withhold the news until twelve weeks had elapsed and at about that point disaster seemed to strike again. Jean went straight to bed and the doctor was called. Dr Benson, the lady doctor at the Kirkby Lonsdale practice, arrived within a few minutes and gave Jean a hormone injection which she hoped would save the situation and indeed it did. Jean had to spend a few more days in bed and Dr Benson returned to repeat the procedure. At this point we had told Jean's parents what was going on and they were very supportive, looking after Jean whilst I was at work. After about a week Jean was up and about again and was a picture of health throughout the rest of the pregnancy.

My sister Marilyn was also pregnant and a little ahead of Jean by a few weeks, so this year there would be three new babies in the family. At this point my mum gave up her job with the school meals service as it had been decided that when Marilyn resumed work, my mum would look after her baby.

In order to keep Gretchen our goat in milk she also had to become pregnant, so when in season we took her in the back of our car to some acquaintances who had a billy goat and lived in Overton, just outside Morecambe. The deed being done, we then transported Gretchen on the return journey to Arkholme, fortunately without any toilet incidents on either leg of the journey.

At work all of my sales staff had gone to evening classes to study for their GCSE in photography and had all passed, each with a grade B. This put me to shame as although I had my trade qualifications, this mainly covered product knowledge. I decided to enrol in the course when it opened in September and when I turned up for the first lesson, the tutor started laughing when he saw me. We went through the syllabus and he said that there was no point in coming to the classes as there was nothing new that he could teach me. The only thing that my work did not cover was photographic history so he told me what I should read to cover that subject. He also told me that I would have to come to classes towards the end of the course to use the darkrooms to process the practical work that I would have to prepare for the examination. Ultimately I passed with a grade A which came as a great relief as I decided that I had to beat my staff to retain my honour.

About this time we received the wonderful news that my sister Marilyn had given birth to Amy Jane so she and Bill at last were parents and our boys had a new little cousin.

In September Andrew started school, really enjoyed it and was reading very well within only a few weeks. We were still involved with the church and by now I had been asked to be on the Arkholme Parish Hall Committee. Jean was on the Arkholme Children's Party Committee, which raised money from a large annual bonfire night and firework display event that we organised. The profits from this paid for a children's Christmas Party which was visited by Santa who gave every child who lived in the village a gift.

After Santa left, the adults organising the party always had a job to stop the older children running out of the hall to try and see where

Santa went. This year these kids were perplexed as seconds later he had disappeared. On this occasion Santa was Bob, the father of Kath Powell, the landlady of the Bay Horse Pub just across the road and Bob was back home and out of sight within about five seconds.

I had started to go to the pub a little more now and popped along for an hour on Christmas Eve. It was always full of people that I knew as I had now been fully accepted as a local and it gave me the opportunity to wish them our season's greetings.

Reg and Andy at Seaton Sluice, September 1973. Photo taken by Jean

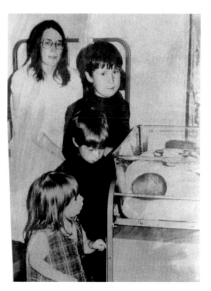

*Introducing Andy, Matt and Claire to
their baby sister Bobbie, September 1980*

Full family picture, 2014. Only the adults are named – Matt far left, Claire next to Matt, Jasmine (Matt's wife) front, Shaun (Claire's husband) rear, Bobbie front, Andy rear, Jean, Reg, and Julia (Andy's wife) far right.

1978

This proved to be a very eventful year with many things going on, beginning with the birth of our daughter Catherine Lucy Claire on 30th January. Jean had gone into labour during the night but things were progressing very slowly. This coincided with the first day of our annual sale at the shop so I had to be there for the opening rush of customers. Shortly after the shop opened we were visited by a representative called Sid Shaverin who sold us batteries, projector lamps and suchlike. When Sid realised my dilemma he volunteered to work in the shop for the day helping Keith, allowing me to go back to the hospital to be with Jean who, after a difficult few hours, eventually gave birth during the mid-afternoon. Our daughter weighed 10lbs and half an ounce, hence the long and difficult labour. We were delighted to have a healthy beautiful daughter who we had named after both of her Great Grandmothers, Catherine and Lucy, but had added Claire because that is the name that we wanted her to be known by. Rearranging the name in any other order did not seem to flow.

I got back to the shop just before closing time and Keith and Sid had experienced a very busy day but had managed fine without me. I am eternally grateful to Sid for his generosity in allowing me to be present at the birth of Claire and was upset and saddened when I heard of his death in 1996. The day after Jean had given birth, and whilst I was visiting her, another mum and her newborn baby were being settled in across the ward from Jean and behind curtains to which I had my back. Eventually the curtains were drawn back and Jean whispered to me to turn around. Imagine my astonishment when I saw Judith with her baby son Stephen. They had just returned from the labour ward and Judith looked very tired but I went across and congratulated her, giving her a peck on the cheek. She looked embarrassed and asked what Jean might think. I told her that Jean was not the jealous sort and would not think that there was anything wrong in me being so pleased to see her, especially as mother and baby were doing well. By now Judith did in fact have an elder daughter of a similar age to Andy so in some respects our lives up to now had seemed to run on parallel lines. Jean's mum and dad looked after the boys whilst Jean was in hospital and after she came out, I took a week off work. Whilst Jean had been in hospital she and Judith had become friends so shortly afterwards a clothes swap was arranged with her giving us girls' clothes and us giving her boys' clothes which our respective children had outgrown.

Now that we had three children, washing our clothes was a challenge and Jean using a dolly tub and posser was no longer an option. We had periodically been using the laundrette but found that we could afford an automatic washing machine, so acquired one, which transformed our lives. We could now also afford a colour television set so pensioned off our now failing black and white set which had been temperamental for some time. I had managed to repair it on the two or three occasions when it had gone wrong but eventually a replacement was the answer.

We had now owned our Datsun Sunny estate car for nearly two years and decided to change it for a new one. Although the model was the same, the shape had been slightly updated and the cost of changing after trading in our old one was very affordable.

At this time the business was doing extremely well but the cost was me having to leave home before the children were out of bed and arriving home after they were asleep. I did have Wednesdays and Sundays off but did all of my bookkeeping at home so only had a limited amount of time that I could spend with the family. Jean was brilliant about this as she too had been brought up in a business family and had seen her father having to devote so much of his time to their market gardening business and knew the sacrifice that had to be made in running a successful business.

Gretchen the goat gave birth to a black and white billy goat. Sadly we could not keep him so after he was three months old got a butcher to come and slaughter him. I assisted and found the whole process highly distressing but the upside was that we had a freezer full of beautiful meat that tasted just like very tender lamb. I am ashamed that it did not turn me into a vegetarian but gave me a great appreciation of what our animals have to go through to satisfy our lust for meat.

One night when watching a holiday programme on television, a timeshare complex in Wales was featured. For the first year only, before the timeshare was put into place, these properties were on weekly lets and looked like they would provide a super holiday. They were, however, too large for just one family so I contacted Marilyn and Bill, who agreed to share with us if we could find a vacant one. After national television coverage I was pessimistic that any would be vacant but when I telephoned the agent the following day was astonished to find that we had a choice, so found a property of perfect dimensions to house all of us.

This was the first year that we did not return to Seahouses but went in the opposite direction, to Aberdovey in Wales. After work on Saturday 9th September, we set off in the most dreadful weather conditions with heavy rain falling for the entire journey. Claire started getting hungry and howled for much of that horrible drive. We were relieved to arrive at last, finding that Marilyn and Bill had got there first, so the lights were all on making our arrival and unpacking easier. Claire was fed and the boys put to bed, followed shortly afterwards by ourselves. We woke up the next morning to a lovely warm and sunny day which set the tone for the entire week that we stayed. We came to an arrangement with Marilyn and Bill to babysit for each other on alternate evenings so every other night we went out. Staying in was not a problem though as after the kids had gone to sleep, we cooked a meal and sat in the large brand new kitchen eating it and demolishing a bottle of wine under the pull down light; it was all very romantic. After seeing what we had done Marilyn and Bill did the same and I think that on the last night we all stayed in and had a wonderful evening together. Each day we explored a different Welsh railway with Claire and the boys, covering the Snowdon Mountain Railway, Talyllyn Railway, Bala Lake Railway and The Festiniog Railway. We all had a wonderful week except Claire who was too young to remember anything.

My brother Fred was now nearing 18 years old and had applied and been accepted to join the RAF Regiment so off he went to RAF Swinderby in Lincolnshire to do his initial training. He seemed to really enjoy it and looked very smart in his RAF uniform. My parents went to his passing out parade and were very proud of him. I had originally agreed to drive them to Lincolnshire but when the time came it was not possible to cross the Pennines by road as every route was blocked by snow; however, the railway had been kept clear so they went by train. When they reached their destination, they got a taxi to the camp with the taxi driver relating to them 'It's a wonderful place, they go in there as boys and come out as men'!

With our family now firmly established we all had Christmas at home. Andy was very excited at the prospect of a visit from Father Christmas, so much so that he stayed awake all night. This put us into something of a quandry so no presents appeared at the end of his bed but instead were left downstairs that year. Andy was quite upset when he thought that Father Christmas had forgotten him but soon cheered up when he got up and came downstairs where the presents for all of the children were waiting for them.

For a little while we had stopped celebrating New Year as our days were always busy and we were tired.

1979

A lthough we did not know it yet, this was going to be the most important year of all to affect our lives.

A few months previously a young couple had moved into Arkholme who kept some livestock including goats. This proved very useful when Gretchen our goat next came into season as we just walked her up the road to be mated. We wanted to keep her in milk so it was essential that she gave birth on a regular basis.

Our village of Arkholme, in conjunction with the neighbouring villages of Gressingham and Whittington, had a monthly newsletter which always began with a page written by our friend George Worthington, the vicar. In what I think was the April edition he had written a particularly inspirationally piece quoting St. Chrysostom, '*God grant me the serenity to accept the things that I cannot change, the courage to change the things I can and the wisdom to know the difference*'. Jean and I were inspired by this as for some time we had wanted to buy our own property but had not really wanted to leave Arkholme. Leaving was the only option, however, as property there was priced way out of our league. We had a long heart to heart conversation one evening and realised that if we lived in Lancaster, it would give our children better opportunities as they became older. The greater choice of schools was the main factor but as they matured, Lancaster offered them the chance to lead what in our opinion would be a more diverse social life. Life in the country was ideal and we were living the dream but at that time there was only one bus a week to and from Lancaster and we realised it would cause frustration to our children when they became teenagers. In Lancaster there was easy access to shops, schools, medical services and such like, so we decided to move.

We started to scour the property pages in the local newspapers and look in estate agents' windows and soon found two properties that we liked. One was in pristine condition and ready to move into, the other was a bit of a wreck and needed a lot of work doing to improve it. The problem was the property that needed all of the work doing was in by far the best location being at the end of a cul-de-sac, next to fields but was still close to town. We contacted the estate agents who told us that there was a lot of interest in this property as it was an ideal family home and properties on this road rarely came onto the market.

As I had the car for work every day, Jean agreed that I should view the property and make an offer there and then if it seemed suitable. I quickly viewed the property, loved the location and despite the bad condition that the house was in, felt that it would be worth the effort to get the house back to a nice family home. After talking to the agents I discovered that the house might be eligible for an improvement grant, which at that time was available from the local authority to generally improve the local housing stock. If eligible, certain conditions would apply, one of them being, whatever money the council gave us, we had at least to match it with our own money.

I contacted the local authority who confirmed that the house would be eligible for an improvement grant but we would have to act quickly as only a certain amount of money was available for each financial year. When that money had all been allocated, one would have to wait for the next financial year to re-apply.

When I first viewed the house I made an offer of £12,995 which was £1000 below the asking price but the agent said that the asking price had already almost been achieved. Jean had still not seen the house but after talking to her we decided to offer the asking price of £13,995 but were told by the agent that in the meantime another party had made the same offer so the property would have to be sold by sealed bid. That meant we and the other party each had to put our bid into an envelope and seal it, the envelopes would both be opened at the same time and whoever had bid the most would have won the bid. We could not afford a lot more so offered £14396. I thought if the other party was in a similar situation to us, they might offer £14395 so that extra pound might make a difference. I will never know what the other party offered but we won the bid and that is all that mattered.

Over the previous seven years, Jean and I had been saving regularly in a building society for this day and when we applied for a mortgage were told that had we not had an account for at least five years, a mortgage would have been out of the question. Everything fell into place very quickly and by the beginning of July we had the keys and Jean at last saw inside our house. I was apprehensive as to what she might think but she, like me, said that the house had a happy atmosphere and despite all that was wrong with it, I had painted an even bleaker picture than had been reality.

Now was the time to tell the wider world of our plans. It was going to take about a year to get the house into a habitable condition so we did have some time on our hands. One Sunday we took the children to see the house and announced that next year this is where we were going to live. Andy burst into tears and said that he would refuse to move, Matt looked gloomy and refused to talk about it and Claire was too young to understand. That was the family reaction to our new start on Cromwell Road. Next we told George Worthington, who at first had a similar reaction of dismay. Jean was still on the Parochial Church Council, I was a sidesman and the whole family were regular churchgoers. We explained to him that it was his article in the village magazine that had inspired us and he said that now he wished he had never written it. He did, however, soon come round, realising that what we had done was best for us.

My parents were delighted as we would only be three streets away from them and I think that Jean's parents were relieved. Rose Cottage was intended to be their retirement home and until we left, they could not retire. They were far too polite to put us under any pressure but after we had announced that we would be leaving Rose Cottage in the summer of 1980, they were quickly putting retirement plans into place.

Gretchen gave birth to twins, Gerda and Billy. Gerda's future was assured but unfortunately Billy was destined for the Freezer. When the time came for the butcher to return, I completely chickened out and left Jean to help him. She coped a lot better than me and I am sure was a lot more useful than I was last time.

Jean had always been interested in the history of Arkholme and in her research found that there had been a charter granting Arkholme permission to have a market and fair 'On the eve, the day and the morrow of St John the Baptist's day'. The charter had been granted in 1280 and Jean thought that as next year would be 1980, a celebration or event of some sort might be appropriate to commemorate the 700th anniversary of the granting of the charter. She firstly spoke to George Worthington on the matter and he also seemed very enthusiastic. They both then suggested the idea to other village people and soon a steering committee was formed as to how an event could be held involving the entire population of the village.

We now had to arrange for the renovation of our house so I contacted a builder friend of mine who said that he could manage the project. He would do all of the building work and knew joiners and plumbers to do the other jobs. We knew two good electricians who were personal friends so they would deal with the electrics. A plan of action was formulated as to in what order the various jobs had to be done, starting with completely stripping the kitchen back to bare brick and digging out the floor.

In the early stages there was little that Jean and I could do at the house so we went off on holiday with her mum and dad. Through a firm called Hoseasons, we had found suitable holiday accommodation in Wales at a holiday park called Glan Gwna in the hamlet of Caeathro, about a mile away from Caernarfon. During the day Jean's parents went off to pursue their own activities and we went off to do ours. We visited more railways, slate quarries and revisited the Blaenau Ffestiniog railway. On the Sunday Jean, Jean's dad and I went to evening worship at the Presbyterian Church in Caernarfon where we were made most welcome. At that time the people of Wales were fighting for greater independence, for their language to be taught in schools and for the Welsh language to be the first language used on all signposts. There was quite a lot of anti-English feeling at that time and we had encountered it now and again. It was so good, therefore, that the congregation of the Presbyterian Church could put all of that aside and their truly Christian attitude and wonderful hospitality made a world of difference to the enjoyment of our holiday.

In September Matthew started school at Arkholme so with both him and Andy at school, Jean had more time with Claire at home during most days. She was busy, however, still growing vegetables and looking after our hens and goats.

Every day before I started work in Lancaster, I went to Cromwell Road to see how the work on our house was progressing and would return at lunchtime if I needed to talk to the builders. In one of our rooms there was a fireplace and Jean and I had debated whether it should stay or go. Jean and I could not agree on this but eventually I won the argument so the fireplace went. The builders said that they needed to know immediately as the fireplace would have to be disposed of with all of the rubble already loaded and ready to go off to the tip. I mentioned that there might be some value in the fireplace on the reclamation market but they assured me that on that particular item there was no value whatsoever. Work on the house gradually progressed so on Sundays towards the end of the year Jean, I and the children came in and started to do what we had to do to the house.

Christmas came and we did not want a repeat performance of Andy staying awake all night again. During the year, I had mentioned to a customer in the shop that we had this problem and he had experienced an identical situation. With a wry grin, he said that every Christmas Eve his children developed a mysterious cough and the best remedy was a dose of Benylin cough medicine which had the side effects of drowsiness. This was a cough medicine that we occasionally used so on Christmas Eve when our boys seemed to develop this sudden and mysterious cough we had the treatment on hand to give them. This did the trick and not only was the cough gone by Christmas morning but they both slept soundly all night.

1980

After Christmas and the New Year had settled down, Jean, I and the family were still spending most Sundays at Cromwell Road. One Sunday towards the end of January it started snowing and became apparent that it would continue for some time. We decided to beat a hasty retreat back to Arkholme but to go via Carnforth and Over Kellet as these roads were always gritted first. This was in preference to our usual route through the village of Halton, which was a shorter route but was more of a minor road. Everything was straightforward until we were halfway up the hill out of the village of Over Kellet. Our car got stuck halfway up the hill and we could neither move forward or backwards. It was still snowing heavily and we were well and truly stuck, the roads had not been gritted and the children were still in the car. We were pondering what to do next when another car slowly drove past us and came to a halt further up the hill. We told the children not to move and Jean and I got out of the car to give assistance to the car ahead. When we reached the car, two young men were out pushing it and their father was driving and with the help of Jean and I, we managed to get it to the top of the hill and just over the brow. At that point the driver got out and with the two young men came back to our car with us. After I got into the driving seat, Jean and the three men pushed our car with me driving it slowly until we reached the hill top. At last we were both in a position to continue and agreed to keep close together until we had to leave them at Arkholme. Even the rest of the journey was not without incident as further down the road, a car coming down a hill to join our road could not stop and demolished the wall of a house next door to the Red Well Inn about two miles out of Arkholme. Our small convoy stopped to offer assistance but the driver was not injured so after helping him to pull his car out of the wall we continued. It was a great relief to arrive back at Rose Cottage and we were so proud of the children who had behaved perfectly during this stressful journey.

Shortly after this event Jean said that she suspected she was pregnant. We had always wanted four children and after accurately planning our first three said that we would let nature take its own course for number four. We were both absolutely delighted but Jean had reservations as to the timing which would be very close to our house move. By an amazing coincidence my sister Marilyn was also pregnant and, as it turned out, only by about three weeks ahead of Jean.

We were spending as much of our spare time as possible at Cromwell Road, decorating and fitting a new kitchen that we had acquired. We had started to get to know a few neighbours who would pop their heads round the door to see how the improvements were progressing. We got invited into their homes and were astonished to see our fireplace fitted in one of our neighbours' front room. They explained that our builders had sold it to them and presumed that we knew. We had trusted our builders and found out that we had been deceived which left us very upset as that trust had been broken. I have not named them but if they ever read this, they will know that we found out and know that they betrayed our trust and we know that they effectively stole our money.

Our next door neighbours, Tom and Barbara Ward, were particularly friendly and it soon became apparent that we were joining a very close knit circle of friends. Back at Arkholme things were hotting up for the 700th anniversary fair celebrations and Jean was getting more heavily involved with finalising the arrangements for a three day medieval event on Friday 19th, Saturday 20th and Sunday 21st June.

The time soon arrived and on Friday evening there was a banquet in the village hall. The theme was on what might have been eaten 700 years before but I can only remember what we had for a starter. That was jellied eels caught locally which were absolutely delicious. Saturday started with great mirth as our milkman, Dave Webster, had donned a jester's outfit, doing his milk round, which put everyone in the right mood for the day. Nearly everyone dressed retrospectively for the occasion with a particularly good selection of yokels and milkmaids. There were stalls near the church and village stocks outside the church gates constructed by Jean's dad. I had gone out the night before putting up direction posters for several miles around the village and beforehand there had been good publicity. As the morning wore on visitors started to arrive and by the afternoon, the village was bustling with people on this beautiful warm sunny day. Sunday was a little quieter and fewer people came but exhibits and decorations were left out until Sunday night when the event finished. As far as I remember a good sum of money was raised which went to the church.

The time had come to get rid of our livestock. My sister Marilyn had some friends who were looking for goats so one Sunday they came to visit us to check out Gretchen and Gerda. They immediately fell in love with them both, so the goats went off to their new home near Tebay. We had decided to kill the hens but true to form I was unable to tackle this so called on the services of my brother-in-law Dick Haston who made short work of the job. As there were twelve hens we had to give several away as there were too many for us to eat and I seem to remember that we kept two with various other family members getting the others. We all enjoyed chicken dinners for a few days afterwards.

We were now in a high state of readiness for our move to Lancaster and had started to move bits and pieces every time we came to decorate. On the 1st August we hired a small removal van and the big move started. Jean and the family stayed at Arkholme to organise our belongings for transportation and I with the help of our nephew Tony Haston shuttled backwards and forwards to Lancaster with all of our things until by late afternoon the move was complete. How we quite managed it I will never know but without the help of Tony it could not have been achieved in such a short time. Jean locked up at Rose Cottage for the last time and drove the family to spend the first night of our new lives in Lancaster.

In 1980 there were nearly 30 children on Cromwell Road so our children quickly made friends and with us having three children most of the activity seemed to gravitate around our house. We constantly had a house full of children but did not mind as they were now the friends of our children who, along with us, had immediately been accepted by our group of wonderful neighbours.

My sister Marilyn gave birth to her second daughter Jill on 13th August so Amy now had a sister.

On 3rd September Jean gave birth to our youngest daughter Roberta Phyllis Margaret (Bobbie) and our family was now complete.

Closure

Between September 1980 and spring 2017 at the time of publication, our family are all now adults with only Bobbie remaining unmarried. Andy is married to Julia and has two daughters, Matthew is married to Jasmine and has one daughter, Claire is married to Shaun and has two sons.

My father died in 1987, Jean's father died in 1998, my mother died in 2009 as already mentioned and Jean's mother died in 2013.

My sister Marilyn went on to have two more children, William and Holly. She has three granddaughters and one grandson. Her husband Bill died in 2005.

My brother Fred left the RAF in the early 1980s and has lived in Germany ever since. He married then later divorced and has two sons and one daughter. His daughter is married with three sons and now lives in Lancaster. One of his sons lives in Morecambe and one still lives in Germany. He also has a stepdaughter who is married with three children.

All of my first cousins and their spouses have now died with the exception of George's wife Mary. She married Eddie Reeds in 1970 and Eddie has since died. Jean and I visit her regularly at her home in

North Shields and she is an amazing 94 years old.

All of my second cousins are alive and well with the exception of Kenneth who died in 2016. All except Phillip are married and have children. Christine also has grandchildren. I am still in regular touch with them all and we periodically all get together at family celebrations.

I have completely lost touch with Rosalind Smaile from Haltwhistle. I know that she married in 1994 but have had no communication from her since 1990 which was the last time that I saw her.

Jean's brother Peter and his wife Ruth were eventually divorced. They had two children Tim and Caroline. Peter is now married to Debbie and they have a daughter, Georgina. Debbie had a daughter Rebecca and a son, Adam to her previous marriage, giving Peter two stepchildren.

Jean's sister Joan is now a widow again. Her son Tony changed his surname from Crawshaw to Haston and is married to Dawn and they have two daughters.

Joan's daughter Suzie is also a widow and has two daughters.

Jean's cousin Robin sadly died at the age of 56 years old. We are still in occasional touch with his widow Judith.

Jean is periodically in touch with her cousins Valerie and Tracy who were bridesmaids at our wedding.

All of my friends' parents have now died with the exception of the ones mentioned here.

We both frequently see Jean's friend Dorothy Skitt who now lives in Preston.

Eric Race died in 1986.

Mrs Robertson died in 1981.

My friend Wesley Oakes died in 1999. I am still in regular touch with his widow Denise.

I am still regularly in touch with David Rack who is married to Olive and lives in Kettering. They have two adult children and grandchildren. David's mother, Irene Rack, is still alive and looks twenty years younger than her wonderful age which I cannot mention, as it is a subject which she prefers to keep secret.

George Worthington died in 2014 but we are still in touch with his widow Margaret.

Silvia Partridge, my mum's wonderful and faithful friend, is still alive and we see her regularly. She is a widow as her husband Jack died in the 1980s. She did re-marry but Richard, her second husband, has now died. Michael, her son, is married to Linda and they have two adult children. Although not mentioned in the book, Sylvia also has a daughter, Dianne.

I often bump into Judith Jackman (nee Hodgson) whilst shopping. This is always a welcome encounter when we update each other on family news which often results in a very long conversation. She is still happily married to her husband Dave.

Pat Hodgson (nee Currie) and Brian are now divorced. Pat has now moved to Australia to be close to her children and grandchildren who emigrated several years ago. I speak to Pat very frequently and we are the best of friends. Brian remained in England and we meet frequently.

Although Phillip Bowker lives reasonably close to me I only see him periodically. He is married to his wife Judith.

Shortly after I started work Margaret Burley died. Eddie, her husband, re-married to an equally wonderful wife. I last saw him shortly before he died, I think in about 2000. I lost touch with his daughter Janice many years ago but continued to see Alison until my retirement in 2014.

I am still in touch with Henry and Barbara Martin who are now retired. Their daughter Christine, a lovely young lady, sadly died in her early forties. After their daughter Alison, they went on to have a third daughter called Lesley, who became a good friend of my sister.

Bill Cowell and his wife Jane live on the Isle of Arran and are now retired. We are in regular contact.

I frequently see Harold James and get updates on his family.

I occasionally see Bill Shand but have lost touch with his brother Robert.

Nellie and Colin Shrimpton moved to Alnwick when Colin became Archivist to The Duke of Northumberland. They still live in Alnwick. Jean and I call in to see them whenever we visit the north east. They are now retired.

All of my teachers mentioned have now died with the exception of Alan Duckles, who is now 84 years old. I still see him frequently.

Len Burch contacted my sister Marilyn in 2010. We have not heard from him since then.

I periodically see Graham Larkin, Gordon Langley and Bill Holden.

John Talbot and his wife Jane (nee Cotchin) divorced but Jean and I remained friendly with them both. Sadly John died in about 2011 and Jane in 2015. We had visited Jane 10 days before her death.

The Rev Booth died shortly after he had baptised Matthew and Rev Noel Coleman died around the year 2000.

Our lovely next door neighbour Barbara Ward died shortly after we moved in to Cromwell Road. Tom Ward lived for a number of years afterwards and became one of our best friends. He sadly died in India whilst on holiday there.

I lost touch with Glen Jackson after Jean and I were married but his father Gordon Jackson, who later left Lancaster, always visited me at the shop when visiting Lancaster until his death around the year 2000.

Ann Whillis is still a close friend of ours and we see her often when visiting Seahouses. Her son Graeme died at the untimely age of 46 years old and we shared her heartbreak. Her younger son Craig is married to Deborah; they live in Craster and have an adult family. Her husband Bart died around 2005 but prior to that they had divorced.

I frequently meet with my great friend Graham Curwen MBE. We have decided to get together on a regular basis to make sure that we keep in touch.

I last saw Eric Rogerson in 2006. He was divorced from his first wife after only two or three years of marriage. He re-married and has an adult family. I have since completely lost touch with him as I have done with his brothers Jimmy and Alan.

Keith Duffy is married to Trish and they have an adult family. I see Keith quite frequently.

Nigel Austin married and had a large family. He died in 2016.

I have completely lost touch with Ken Ward and Lorina Bell (nee Stavert).

We are still very close to our great friends Dave and Carol Silver (nee Lofthouse). We meet regularly and do family things together. They have a son Stuart who lives in Glasgow and a daughter Catherine who lives in Lancaster with her husband James. Catherine is expecting a baby in May but by then, this book will be with the publisher. I wish her and James great happiness for the future with their new baby.

Oh yes, I nearly forgot to tell you an important story. In about 1996, I attended a lecture by a local historian called Mrs Nelson on the subject of 'The History of Retailing in Lancaster'. She went back in history of how farmers and weavers brought their goods to market and how retailing began, right up to the onset of present day stores and supermarkets. She explained that when we had an abundance of small shops up to the 1950s, shopkeepers had indentured apprentices but that had mainly died out and by 1960, indentured apprenticeships in their retail speciality no longer existed.

I had been asked to give a vote of thanks and started my thanks with the statement, 'As an indentured retail apprentice, starting in 1962, I would like to thank you ...'. After my vote of thanks, an astonished Mrs Nelson came and asked me if I really had started my apprenticeship in 1962 which I confirmed.

She then said to me, 'YOU MUST HAVE BEEN THE VERY LAST APPRENTICE, IN RETAILING, IN LANCASTER,' hence the title of my book, The Last Apprentice.

My thanks go to Stephen Dixon for designing the cover of my book, my son Matthew for layout suggestions, and to Andy, Claire and Bobbie for making me stop at 1980, in the hope that the reader has not been too bored and managed to finish my story.